LOSING OUR
VOICE

Alain Saulnier

LOSING OUR VOICE

Radio-Canada Under Siege

Translated by Pauline Couture

DUNDURN
TORONTO

Translator: Pauline Couture
Copy editor: Andrea Waters
Design: Jennifer Gallinger
Cover design: Laura Boyle
Printer: Webcom

Library and Archives Canada Cataloguing in Publication

Saulnier, Alain
[Ici était Radio-Canada. English]
    Losing our voice : Radio-Canada under siege / Alain Saulnier ; Pauline Couture, translator.
Translation of: Ici était Radio-Canada.

Includes bibliographical references and index.
Issued in print and electronic formats.
ISBN 978-1-4597-3315-2 (paperback).--ISBN 978-1-4597-3316-9
(pdf).--ISBN 978-1-4597-3317-6 (epub)

    1. Canadian Broadcasting Corporation--History. 2. Public
television--Government policy--Canada. 3. Public radio--
Government policy--Canada. 4. Public broadcasting--Canada--
History. I. Couture, Pauline, 1954-, translator II. Title.
II. Title: Ici était Radio-Canada. English.

HE8689.9.C3S2913 2015   384.5406'571   C2015-905152-5
                                         C2015-905153-3

1 2 3 4 5   19 18 17 16 15

We acknowledge the support of the **Canada Council for the Arts** and the **Ontario Arts Council** for our publishing program. We also acknowledge the financial support of the **Government of Canada** through the **Canada Book Fund** and **Livres Canada Books**, and the **Government of Ontario** through the **Ontario Book Publishing Tax Credit** and the **Ontario Media Development Corporation**. In addition, we acknowledge the financial support of the **Government of Canada** through the **National Translation Program for Book Publishing**, an initiative of the **Roadmap for Canada's Official Languages 2013–2018: Education, Immigration, Communities**, for our translation activities.

VISIT US AT
Dundurn.com | @dundurnpress | Facebook.com/dundurnpress | Pinterest.com/dundurnpress

Dundurn
3 Church Street, Suite 500
Toronto, Ontario, Canada
M5E 1M2

TABLE OF CONTENTS

In memory of my mother, Yvannette,
who left us during the writing of this book,
and to the love of my life, Dominique,
and to our daughter, Léa

PREFACE

This book deals with the threats to CBC/Radio-Canada today and documents the problems that have been present throughout its history. When I first wrote the book, I was speaking to a francophone audience and I concentrated on the history of the French networks that had been at the heart of most of my professional life. The cultural references in the book testify to this.

But I also believe that English-speaking Canadians will find it interesting to see the impact of Quebec-Canada tensions on the relationship between the federal government and the public broadcaster.

Whether it was under John Diefenbaker's Progressive Conservatives or during the Pierre Trudeau, Brian Mulroney, or Jean Chrétien years, Radio-Canada has always been under great pressure, and the government has always tried to bend the public broadcaster to its will. Public broadcaster or state broadcaster? That is the question at the heart of the debate, particularly when the sovereigntist movement was at its height in Quebec. Pierre Trudeau seriously considered shutting down Radio-Canada. The question remains entirely relevant today, as we examine the fall out from Stephen Harper's efforts to asphyxiate the public broadcaster.

Whether we are francophones or anglophones, we share the good fortune of having a public broadcaster that is one of the most important institutions for the health of our democracy. We are also fortunate that the exemplary BBC model inspired the original drafters of the founding statutes that created CBC/Radio-Canada.

This book had a major impact in Quebec when it first appeared and at the time of my appearance on the popular television show *Tout le monde en parle* (*Everybody's Talking About It*). Two weeks later, thousands of people marched in the streets of Montreal in support of Radio-Canada. But what is happening on the CBC side of things? Readers have convinced me that this story was worth telling to an English-speaking public — largely because we share so much of the same story. CBC and Radio-Canada face the same challenges to their survival; the digital era is creating great upheaval in media consumption habits, and at the same time there is not enough support for the public broadcaster among the political class in this country.

This book is a passionate plea for the maintenance and the defence of CBC/Radio-Canada in the twenty-first century.

Alain Saulnier, June 2015

ACKNOWLEDGEMENTS

I want to thank all who have shared their memories, insights, and confidences with me. Some of them are named in the text, while others have preferred to remain anonymous. I have been able to write this book because of their support and collaboration. I particularly want to thank the former minister of communications, the late Marcel Masse, a friend of CBC/Radio-Canada with whom I was able to have several long conversations a few weeks before his death in August 2014.

I also owe a special thanks to Professor Pierre Pagé for the portion of this book that covers the years prior to the beginning of the television services; to Renaud Gilbert, former director of le Réseau de l'information (RDI), for the many documents that he has taken great care to preserve and to which he gave me access; and to the family of the late Raymond David, former vice-president of Radio-Canada, who shared his archives with me.

I also want to thank my valued colleague and dear friend, Geneviève Guay, without whom this book would never have seen the light of day. She often challenged me, but her advice was always sound.

I want to extend a special thanks to Pauline Couture, who translated the book. We share the same passion for CBC and Radio-Canada.

Finally, thank you to my spouse, Dominique, for her unfailing support and her critical input on the text in its various iterations.

INTRODUCTION

I don't know a single prime minister of Canada who hasn't tried, at one time or another, to muzzle the journalists at Radio-Canada.

— Solange Chaput-Rolland,
author, journalist, senator

On Wednesday, February 22, 2012, I left the Centre d'information, the area in Radio-Canada's Montreal headquarters that houses News and Current Affairs. I was headed for the twelfth-floor office of the new vice-president of French Services, Louis Lalande. I had asked for the meeting to deal with an issue at our all-news network, RDI.

Upon my arrival, he asked me to follow him into the boardroom — which I did, unconcerned. As soon as I saw that the vice-president of human resources was waiting for us there, I understood what was about to take place. This was the day I would be fired — after fifteen years as an executive, the last six as managing director of News and Current Affairs in French Services.

The next day, as I entered the newsroom, many employees protested the decision to fire me with sustained applause that was heard live on-air through the open microphones of the onsite RDI anchor desk. Senior management didn't like it one bit.

Why had I been fired when things were going rather well in News and Current Affairs? Was the decision driven by a political command? I asked myself that question, among many others. And I wanted to know more.

I decided to research the reasons for my firing. This led me to take a broader look at the relationship between the public broadcaster and the Canadian government. I discovered that the relationship has always been complex, and sometimes fraught with tension. I felt it was a story that deserved to be told.

At the same time, along with many others, I am disgusted by the deliberate asphyxiation and dismantling of CBC/Radio-Canada.

Many people, conscious of the looming danger, have asked me to speak up. I have written this book primarily in the hope that I can contribute to saving our national public broadcaster.

My professional relationship with Radio-Canada began in 1984, when I was first hired as a casual journalist. This meant being on standby to replace full-time staff journalists in the newsroom as needed. I remember the exact moment I started, just after my birthday in January. What a great birthday present that was! I remember it as if it were yesterday, grinning like an idiot as I crossed the threshold of Montreal's Maison de Radio-Canada for the first time. I would be working as a journalist at Radio-Canada, the greatest journalistic institution in the country! My hiring was unhoped-for, as I had come to the profession after a long and circuitous route.

I dragged my feet career-wise before choosing journalism. I had started by investing my youthful energy into a far-left youth group, the Communist Marxist-Leninist League. It may be useful to remember that in the 1970s, left-wing groups helped part of my generation to get their start in life and in society. For the previous generation of Quebeckers, that of Gérard Pelletier, Jean Marchand, and Jeanne Sauvé, the groups that fostered this sense of belonging were Catholic student and youth groups such as Jeunesse ouvrière catholique or Jeunesse étudiante catholique. In the Quebec of my generation, as in many European countries, left-wing groups introduced many young people to the idea of social engagement.

This is not the place for an exhaustive review of Marxism, which I left behind long ago, nor is it a story of the long detour that eventually brought me to journalism. Suffice it to say that there came a day when I understood that it was time to choose between activism and journalism, and that for me the choice was clear. As long as I could remember, becoming a journalist had been my deepest desire.

It was my extraordinary good fortune to practise the profession I had chosen inside the most important media outlet for francophones in this country, Radio-Canada.

I worked there for nearly thirty years: first in regional television news in Montreal, then as a reporter on the desk and on the street. Then I moved from television news to current affairs programs, particularly *Le Point*, which followed the nightly national newscast, *Le Téléjournal*. I worked as a researcher, a segment producer, and coordinating producer responsible for studio-based interviews.

In the fall of 1992, as *Le Téléjournal* was going through some changes, I left Radio-Canada for just over two years to work at Radio-Québec, the provincial educational television network. Sometime in the summer of 1995, I returned to Radio-Canada with the feeling of coming home.

I felt the pride of belonging to a great institution. Then, after having been a producer in television, I left the rank of unionized employee in 1997 to join management as head of Radio News. Two years later, I became director of Radio News and Current Affairs. Finally, in June 2006, the vice-president of French-language Services, Sylvain Lafrance, asked me to take on overall management of News and Current Affairs for both radio and television. This was the position in which I remained until my unsolicited departure in 2012.

Radio-Canada, a Family History

As long as I can remember, my life, along with that of my family, has been linked to Radio-Canada.

In 1952, a few days before Christmas, my father and my oldest brother walked down Mount Royal Avenue in Montreal, finishing up the Christmas shopping. That year, all of those who strolled along Mount Royal stopped in front of one particular display window. My father had to carve out a space for his seven-year-old son to join the admirers of the desired object. Prominently displayed was the novelty of the year, a television set. For the first time, often live, we could watch actors and artists move, dance, and sing. *La boîte à images* had come to life — a fantastic window into the worlds of reality and imagination! For months, we had talked about nothing else. My two older brothers, like other children from Avenue des Cèdres in Cité-Jardin, had even experienced the privilege of watching *Pépinot et Capucine*[1] at the house of our neighbour, Monsieur Jean. He was the first one on our street to acquire this marvellous invention. "Panpan always wins!" the chorus of children would shout at the screen.

My father knew, a few days before that unforgettable Christmas in 1952, that he was making history by buying the television set. From that Christmas Day on, television was part of the Saulnier family. At last, Pépinot, Capucine, the Bear, Monsieur Blanc, and Monsieur Potiron[2] entered into our family universe; soon, they would be known to all of Quebec's children.

On the first Saturday night after the purchase of the television set, the family was comfortably installed in the living room to watch the hockey game between the Canadiens and the Detroit Red Wings. At the time, hockey started at 9:00 p.m on television, while the live game began an hour earlier at the Forum. From the beginning of the game, there was action and excitement, especially if Maurice Richard had just scored.

On January 1, 1953, my mother, pregnant with her fourth child, watched the first televised year-end review, *Variétés 52*, the ancestor of today's traditional *ByeBye*. Comfortably ensconced in the living room, she could finally put faces on her favourite radio stars: Juliette Béliveau, Paul Berval, Roger Garceau, and Juliette Huot. She confided in me that she had laughed throughout the show, rocking the world of her unborn baby.

A few weeks later, the cries of a newborn upset the household's television habits. It was my turn to join the family. In fact, you could call me a child of television.

Until January 1954, Radio-Canada's television offered bilingual programming, an approach that would be entirely impossible today. The perfectly bilingual Franco-Manitoban host, Henri Bergeron, read the news in English at certain hours and in French at other times. Obviously, this setup heightened everyone's frustrations!

Introduction

From the beginning, television disrupted listening habits for radio, the first mass medium, which had to adjust to this invasive newcomer. The fear was that once television was a familiar fixture in family living rooms, it would simply spell the end of radio. On Radio-Canada television's launch night, the journalist/host Judith Jasmin celebrated the birth of television, of course, but she also worried about its impact on radio. Fortunately, no one thought of discarding radio, which proved to have an almost mythical ability to adapt to technological change. It was radio that had laid the foundation of public service in this country in 1936. In peacetime and in war, Radio-Canada's radio service was a priceless jewel for francophones from coast to coast. It made an enormous contribution to who we are. Its history, however, has not been entirely without challenges. CBC/Radio-Canada has always been at the heart of conflicts and crises. Wherever you have a public service funded by the federal government, you can be sure that in turn, the political powers will always be tempted to act as owners and constantly try to impose their point of view. To be sure, the temptation is strong. Nevertheless, the Broadcasting Act provides for the independence of CBC/Radio-Canada.[3]

By law, Radio-Canada is a public service and not a state broadcaster. This important distinction means that it must serve the public first, not the state. The British, who created the BBC model, defined the distance that must be maintained between the government and the public service as the arm's-length relationship. This is consistent with the well-known legal concept of the arm's-length principle, which characterizes a transactional relationship in which each party is independent and on an equal footing.

In search of the autonomy and independence from political interference that the Act promises, CBC/Radio-Canada has struggled with an ambiguous and sometimes conflict-ridden relationship with political power.

Of course, the federal government wields a big stick: under the same act, it votes on CBC/Radio-Canada's operating budget.

It would be naive to believe that this kind of tension is unique to our country. On the contrary, ambiguity is common in the western countries that have public television services. In this country, however, the deep division in public opinion on the national question has certainly added to the difficulty of the relationship between the public broadcaster and the government.

Of course, Radio-Canada's problems have not been confined to tension with the federal government. There are other kinds of struggles that must be discussed, such as the problems with private radio and television services. The private sector was not well disposed towards the creation of a public service and to subsequent competition and cohabitation with it.

There have also been tensions in the population served, between francophones in Quebec and those in the rest of Canada, reflecting a kind of collision of identities within the country. On occasion, political parties have successfully exploited these collisions.

And obviously, the public broadcaster's English-language networks have also had their own difficulties in their relationship with political power.

In this book, I have, in passing, evoked some of the major episodes of these sagas; I will leave to others the detailed telling of them. I intend to concentrate mostly on the particular relationship between the French services of Radio-Canada and the federal political power, notably from my personal experience. I do not profess to cover Radio-Canada's history exhaustively. I will examine certain periods more closely, including that of Pierre Elliott Trudeau's Liberals, and, after 2006, that of Stephen Harper's Conservatives.

I also want to emphasize that this book does not constitute an attack on any particular government. I am not involved in partisan politics. My purpose is rather to make a plea for the maintenance of an arm's-length relationship between the public broadcaster and the government of the day. The role of CBC/Radio-Canada is precisely to make known, freely, the range and diversity of opinions that make up society. This is what constitutes its strength and its unique identity in the media spectrum.

Finally, a last and important clarification before getting to the meat of the topic: the great majority of journalists and managers who have worked in Radio-Canada's News and Current Affairs Services have always believed that their mission was to inform the public correctly, according to the professional norms of their respective eras. Each, in their way, has fiercely defended their independence. They deserve our gratitude.

Despite everything I am preparing to lay out today, I remain an unconditional supporter of public broadcasting, and I am convinced that the confidence the population has always placed in the institution is largely well founded.

I want to share this work with all those I have loved and who have supported me, no doubt because we shared the same passion for quality of information, the same commitment that Radio-Canada espouses. And of course, I want to offer it to a few people who loved me less. It will keep them busy.

CHAPTER 1

Beginnings

The first real public radio service worthy of the name in the Montreal area was not Radio-Canada, but rather CKAC, which also owned the daily newspaper *La Presse* at the time. In 1922, CKAC became the first mass radio station for francophones. It was among the first radio stations in the country to offer classical music concerts, operas, and operettas. The station even had its own symphony orchestra, which tells you everything you need to know! Between 1929 and 1939, CKAC broadcast *L'Heure provinciale* (*The Provincial Hour*), a very audacious cultural and socioeconomic magazine for its time, helmed by Édouard Montpetit, the secretary-general of l'Université de Montréal. The program, funded by the Government of Quebec, offered CKAC's audience hundreds of lectures on the economy and was immensely successful.

Later on, CKAC developed a literature program with author Robert Choquette and aired classical theatrical plays. Such programming was a reflection of the station's first general manager, Jacques-Narcisse Cartier.[1] But this exemplary programming on CKAC was also the result of close collaboration between Cartier and the head of programming at the time, Joseph-Arthur Dupont.[2] It was Dupont who had enriched the programming by negotiating an agreement with the CBS network that provided access to symphony concerts from many other cities with orchestras of their own. In 1932, four years before the creation of CBC/Radio-Canada, Minister of Marine Alfred Duranleau, who was responsible for communications, asked Dupont to leave CKAC to join the Canadian Broadcasting Commission, the organizational ancestor of

CBC/Radio-Canada. Its mandate included the functions of the future Canadian Radio-television and Telecommunications Commission (CRTC). The commission broadcast radio programs and gave birth to CBC/Radio-Canada in 1936. From the beginning of the public service, Dupont was the director of French-language programs on Radio-Canada,[3] which therefore became a kind of descendent of CKAC.

Professor Pierre Pagé, of l'Université du Québec à Montréal, has summarized the role of CKAC by saying that it was "private radio in the spirit of public service.... From the beginning, radio appeared to be a medium centred on the quality of sound, closely tied to the art of music. Montreal's best artists came to interpret classical music live, every two days."[4] My mother told me that her family, the Poiriers, had rapidly adopted CKAC. It is not surprising, given that singing and classical music were almost sacred in her family. Nothing brought her more joy than attending the free classical music concerts in Lafontaine and Molson parks in Montreal. It was the loveliest possible family outing. So now, to be able to listen to concerts and arias from operas on radio — what an opportunity!

A few years later, when Radio-Canada's radio service launched, my mother became a faithful and avid listener — once again because of her love of music — when the network began to broadcast the Metropolitan Opera from New York.

CBC/Radio-Canada's radio services were created in 1936 precisely to counter the powerful cultural domination of the United States. It was a way for Canada to distinguish itself from its powerful neighbour to the south. At the same time, the public broadcaster offered the Canadian government a platform to address all Canadian citizens, from coast to coast, anytime.

In so doing, Canada was affirming its own identity and territory.

One of those who played a formative role in the creation of public radio was Graham Spry, cofounder of the Canadian Radio League. His writing and his actions promoted public awareness of this avant-garde idea. Thanks to the league's pressure on both Conservative and Liberal elected officials, William Lyon Mackenzie King's government was persuaded to create a public broadcasting system that would contribute to building the Canada of the future. In this sense, Graham Spry was one of the visionaries of the twentieth century. On the francophone side, the seminal role was played by Joseph-Arthur Dupont, father of the first French-language radio programming.

These early beginnings were not uneventful. Some private radio companies were not at all happy to see the arrival of CBC/Radio-Canada in their markets. The tensions between CBC/Radio-Canada and the private broadcasters are not new. They have always been there, as long as the public broadcaster has existed. We will come back to this.

The Mandate

At the outset, it was necessary to define a mandate for the national public broadcaster. What link should there be between the Canadian government and CBC/Radio-Canada? According to broadcast historian Pierre Pagé, this philosophical debate was not front and centre; the founders were simply too busy with the practical and logistical aspects of the operation. On the important matter of the independence of the public broadcaster, the most natural solution was to turn to the existing British model: the BBC. What could be simpler than to import it wholesale? The idea was even more obvious because the first president of CBC/Radio-Canada was British and had brought with him the only model he knew. Ever since, generations of employees and managers at the public broadcaster have taken inspiration from the BBC model and used it as a reference.

Since Canada has two major language groups, francophone and anglophone, another fundamental question that arose at the outset was whether the service should be bilingual and broadcast from a single source or whether it should have two signals, with distinctive programming from each. Should there be a single management or one for francophone Canada and one for anglophone Canada? These questions remain relevant today.

The Canadian Radio Commission's pre-1936 experience of radio broadcasting had allowed it to test certain programming models. The preferred model at the outset was a bilingual service with shared programming. Of course, all this was well before the debates on bilingualism in Canada and on the place of French in Quebec. However, both francophones and anglophones made it clear that they wanted their own programming. Pierre Pagé tells a relevant story: before 1936, the Canadian Radio Commission's bilingual radio programming featured the Lionel Daunais Lyrical Trio. Anglophone listeners complained in large numbers about Lionel Daunais's French-language songs. Although this now seems obvious, at the time it came as a surprise that anglophone and francophone audiences have very different tastes!

Several years before the creation of the public broadcaster, the Aird Commission had recommended the creation of a Crown corporation to operate a national broadcasting system. At the time of its adoption, the Broadcasting Act provided for the creation of a public corporation made up of two distinct entities: Radio-Canada for francophones and the CBC for anglophones. We can therefore assume that at the time of the creation of the "national" public broadcaster, there was a clear political intent to reflect the specific needs of each language group.

There were two significant developments related to the autonomy of the French-language network in relation to the CBC. The first was in January 1941, when Assistant Director-General Augustin Frigon inaugurated the Radio-Canada News Service and chose Marcel Ouimet to lead it. This was a meaningful decision, a way to affirm the editorial independence of French-language radio. Up to that point, French radio had been limited to the translation of items from newsrooms in Toronto and Winnipeg. The only other source of news at that time was the Canadian Press, which offered English-language services only.

The second important development was the launch, in October 1941, of Radio-Collège, an entity with equal status to the News Service inside Radio-Canada. During wartime, when censorship was in full force, Radio-Collège was a bastion of freedom for francophone culture, unlike the rest of the program schedule, which was largely controlled by the government.

Once again taking inspiration from Great Britain, Augustin Frigon and his colleague, professor and producer Aurèle Séguin, had modelled Radio-Collège on the BBC's educational radio service. This entirely new programming carved out a space where Radio-Canada's creators and artisans could work freely. It was more independent because it was not subject to the News Service's obligations to support the war effort, nor to censorship and propaganda. Here, I salute the artisans of Radio-Collège, who contributed to the shaping of French-Canadian identity and the emerging Québécois identity. This recognition is necessary and long overdue, as we have too often given all the credit to Radio-Canada's television service for having played this major role in the development of culture and cultural identity among francophones. Well before the dawn of television, Radio-Collège had been showing the way since 1941.

The News Service and the Second World War

CKAC had also opened the way for francophones in news and current affairs; since 1938, Albert Duquesne had read newscasts written by CKAC's thirty-odd journalists. The private station had beaten Radio-Canada to the punch in creating a true radio news service. It is interesting to note that CKAC served not only Montreal, but the entire province of Quebec. This forced Radio-Canada to develop an expansion strategy within Quebec at the same time as it was creating a coast-to-coast service.

Competing with CKAC in Quebec also accelerated the obligation for the public broadcaster to offer programming specifically designed for francophones, and therefore to dissociate itself from a common approach with CBC's English-language services.

One landmark event in the relationship between Radio-Canada and the government of the day happened on September 10, 1939. That day, Prime Minister Mackenzie King broadcast his radio address announcing Canada's entry into the war against Nazi Germany separately in each of the country's two main languages. Although those who had been arguing in favour of this approach had barely dared to hope for success, the prime minister legitimized the idea of autonomous programming in French for Radio-Canada.

After two years at war in Europe, the need to do a better job of informing the population from coast to coast about the Canadian armed forces' activities in Europe was becoming increasingly obvious; this sparked the creation of the Radio-Canada News Service.

In addition to the declaration of war, Mackenzie King also announced the simultaneous imposition of censorship for all Canadian media. It was henceforth forbidden to speak or to write independently. All were subject to censorship on all matters related to the war. The arm's-length principle between Radio-Canada and the federal government had therefore become an intellectual conceit by 1942, when the Canadian government organized a plebiscite on conscription. In an article headlined "La censure en temps de guerre: Radio-Canada et le plebiscite de 1942" ("Censorship in Wartime: Radio-Canada and the plebiscite of 1942"),[5] Alain Canuel says Radio-Canada management blacklisted the opponents of conscription in 1942, while those who were favourable to conscription could express themselves at will — all this in support of national unity. Radio-Canada was certainly not alone in having to deal with these new rules. The National Film Board of Canada (NFB) was also subject to the federal government's determination to support the Canadian Army's war effort. A number of films from this time are available on the NFB's website. Today, these productions would be seen as unmistakable examples of government propaganda. They include animated films from the NFB's legendary Norman McLaren,[6] notably a campaign film for the famous Victory Bonds, which helped to finance Canada's war effort.

The people who lived through the Second World War remember these patriotic messages created by the NFB and presented on neighbourhood movie screens.

On radio, the great hero among war correspondents was Marcel Ouimet. Perfectly bilingual, he produced reports for both the French and English networks. It was he, in 1943, who sent the news from the front where Canadian soldiers were engaged. Two years later, Radio-Canada International (RCI) began to broadcast. From 1946, its airwaves became home to a certain René Lévesque, back from the front where he had also worked — not for Radio-Canada, but for the Voice of America radio service.

Lévesque had accompanied the U.S. Army in its battles and travels in Europe. In his memoirs, he tells the emotional story of his arrival at Dachau, shortly after American troops had liberated the last surviving Jewish prisoners in the concentration camp.

When Canada participated in the Korean War in 1950, it was again René Lévesque who reported for RCI. Some of these reports are available on the CBC archives website.[7] It was here that he developed his great talent for clear communications and popularization, which would make him a celebrity when he moved to television a few years later.

The Golden Age of Radio

Some people think of the Second World War period as the golden age of radio. This is first and foremost because all families wanted news from the front, but there is another reason: it was also the time of the emergence of the *radioromans* — radio soap operas beloved by my mother's and my grandmother's generations. At home, they listened to *Rue principale* (*Main Street*)[8] and *Un homme et son péché* (*A Man and His Sin*).[9] The collective experience of these radio soaps and their imaginary universes reinforced a sense of belonging among francophones. It defined the cultural and national identity of French Canada. Furthermore, Radio-Collège's programming offered forays into the history of humanity and the world of ideas.

At the same time, English Canadians were building a national identity of their own, one more and more Canadian and less and less British. This search for an English-Canadian identity was nearly always set in the context of distinguishing themselves from American culture.

CBC/Radio-Canada, then, served to forge national identity for both francophones and anglophones in this country. There were two identities, each struggling with their own particular challenges. (At the time, most people were completely unaware of the existence of Acadian or Aboriginal identities.)

Following my parents' generation, mine had to pick up the continuing thread of this search for cultural identity. The first *Un homme et son péché* aired on radio, but the story was then adapted for television for the following generation under the title *Les Belles Histoires des pays d'en haut* (*Beautiful Stories from the Upper Country*). It is still possible to connect with this cultural heritage when the *Belles Histoires* series reappears on cable from time to time.

Once again, private broadcasters were the first to offer radio soaps. It was often difficult to distinguish between the private and public versions of this kind of radio programming. In fact, it was not unusual at the time for broadcasters to raid their competitors for talent across public-private lines, especially the big names. This was the case for Roger Baulu, who was known as the "Prince of Announcers." He first achieved stardom on CKAC. Well before he hosted *La Poule aux œufs d'or* (*The Hen with the Golden Eggs*)[10] on Radio-Canada television, Baulu had anchored radio game shows such as *La Course aux trésors* (*The Treasure Hunt*). His departure for Radio-Canada at the beginning of the war had provoked an uproar and heightened the rivalry between CKAC and Radio-Canada. Baulu spent a large part of his professional life at Radio-Canada. He enjoyed a brilliant career there as a host, first on radio and then on television, where he co-hosted (with Jacques Normand) the famous late-night talk show *Les Couche-tard*[11] from 1960 to 1970.

Right after the hockey game on Saturday night, as a child, I was allowed to stretch out the evening by a few minutes. Lying on the floor in front of the family television set with my older brothers, I allowed myself to be rocked to sleep by the show's theme song, written by Jean-Pierre Ferland:

> Regardez-les, les couche-tard, ils ont l'œil lourd et gris
> Ils traînent le jour, les couche-tard, et poussent la nuit
> Ils vivent au soleil de minuit et on les arrose au whisky,
> ces fleurs de macadam …
> [Look at the late-to-bed crowd, eyes heavy and grey,
> They drag themselves around all day and grow at night,
> They live under the midnight sun and are watered with
> whisky, these flowers of the tarmac …]

These words still resonate today among my childhood memories. I loved going to bed late and playing with the older kids in the family.

CHAPTER 2

Temporary Difficulties

Television had a spectacular impact on people's lives. Family life was considerably transformed, because television had an immense attraction and was an extraordinary beacon, a rallying point. It imposed its schedule and its rhythm on our lives. Mealtime for a family of six children such as ours was always compressed by the television schedule. The children would rush to eat their after-school snack to be on time for their heroes in *La Boîte à surprises* (*Surprise Box*) or for Luc and Luce from *Opération mystère* (*Operation Mystery*).[1] Our eyes were religiously fixed on the small screen. At the same time, the adults were discovering *Les Belles Histoires des pays d'en haut*. This series had such a powerful hold on the collective imagination that it sometimes created confusion between fiction and Quebec's historical reality.

In a very real way, the society to which my parents belonged was being revealed to them. Indeed, the magical picture-box offered them a very flattering self-image. And what a gift for French-speaking people! We owe the rise in awareness of our collective identity to the eruption of television in our lives. The francophone public discovered strong personalities such as Pierre Trudeau, a founder of *Cité libre* magazine, who dared to challenge the absolute power of the Catholic church in a 1957 debate on a show called *Prise de bec*.[2] Or Gérard Filion, director of the newspaper *Le Devoir*, who vigorously called out members of the Maurice Duplessis government implicated in the 1958 natural gas scandal.[3]

Television also showed people in action, going about their lives; it offered a cultural identity, and it put a face on national pride. People of immense talent — such as the great singer-songwriter Félix Leclerc — came, each in their own way, to express our culture and, at the same time, make us aware of its value. This empowered francophones to be proud and also reassured them, despite their minority status within Canada. Jean-Pierre Desaulniers,[4] a keen observer of media influence, discussed this phenomenon in *L'Actualité* magazine in 2002:

> … in most of the world's countries, the collective imagination has been nourished essentially by a national literature and film…. In Quebec, this happened largely through television — because it came along exactly when Quebec society had a great need to modernize its identity.[5]

Obviously, part of the reason that people of my generation are attached to Radio-Canada is that it had a monopoly on the airwaves in Montreal for a decade before the 1961 arrival of its competitor, Télé-Métropole. In fact, we had no choice: there was only one French-language station! Radio-Canada had no need to get audience numbers from BBM or any other firm.

Its television service was virtually alone in building a cultural identity. In this sense, Radio-Canada's monopoly did a great job of spreading the culture and the ideas that subsequently shaped Quebec's Quiet Revolution. Still today, the cultural identity of Quebec's francophones is largely founded on this legacy. Some observers do bring a more subtle understanding of this picture. Speaking about Radio-Canada's influence, Jean-Pierre Desaulniers added,

> While Radio-Canada's artisans were open-minded, they were also mostly Outremont intellectuals who had studied with the Jesuits, and had been infected with their haughtiness towards the people…. As soon as the people were able to have a more egalitarian relationship with their television service, they were quick to take advantage of the opportunity.[6]

Bilingual Television

In the beginning, public television was a reflection of the Canada of its time. Radio-Canada's employees had to swear an oath of allegiance to the queen in order to work there, a practice that was discreetly abandoned in the early 1970s. All correspondence and even the paycheques were produced in English only. Radio-Canada was a reflection of the place of francophones within Canada. From 1952 to 1954, Radio-Canada offered bilingual programming on a single feed, Channel 2. This definitely did not meet the expectations of francophone society at the time. Bilingualism was not very widespread, except among francophones outside Quebec, and that was mostly out of obligation. No one today would dare to propose such a "bilingual" television service.

It is worth mentioning that a similar idea reappeared briefly in 1992. During the presidency of Gérard Veilleux, CBC Newsworld, the English network's all-news service, applied to the CRTC for permission to translate four hours of prime-time programming a day into French for cable companies serving francophone audiences. The professional association representing Quebec journalists, la Fédération professionnelle des journalistes du Québec (FPJQ), of which I was president at the time, was firmly against the idea:

> Newsworld's translation proposal cannot be the all-news service that francophones expect. Equality between francophones and anglophones in this country, and senior management of the CBC has to know this, is the opposite of sub-titling and translation! It consists of equal status for the two peoples.[7]

Happily, the application was rejected. Three years later, on January 1, 1995, RDI, Radio-Canada's own all-news network, finally launched.

But let us go back to the beginnings of television. In 1954, the francophones in Radio-Canada's senior management were anxious to liberate themselves from the yoke of the bilingual service and to take charge of their own programming. The struggle for Radio-Canada's autonomy vis-à-vis CBC was just beginning. The management of Radio-Canada's French-language services has always had to fight to preserve its share of the overall CBC/Radio-Canada budget. Over the years, this share of the budget has varied between 35 and 40 percent. Today the separation of the budgets is still fundamental, because it allows francophones to establish distinct programming with free agency. For francophone staff, it was a matter of finding their own space within an organization that was run by anglophones.

The Producers' Strike

In their own way, the producers of French-language programs joined this search for independence in 1959.

December 5, 1958, marked the beginning of a long producers' strike. They were demanding the right to unionize, a prospect that was anathema to the Conservative government of John Diefenbaker. But this was not just a labour conflict. The battle between the producers and management was also a struggle for independent programming for francophone audiences. This was one of the objectives behind the request for union accreditation. Under the circumstances, the government of the day was quite willing to let the conflict fester. For three long months, CBC/Radio-Canada management sent only unilingual anglophones to the bargaining table. This speaks volumes about the relative weight of francophones in senior management at the time.

In an interview with me on Radio-Canada in 1986, René Lévesque said,

> In Ottawa, the minister of labour, Michael Starr, allowed the conflict to drag on, and all the while, during the strike, Radio-Canada was showing the best French films available, making us all mutter profanities on the picket line....[8]

It is certainly reasonable to speculate that the conflict would not have lasted as long if it had been employees at CBC, instead of Radio-Canada, who had gone on strike. This view was certainly shared by

Radio-Canada host René Lévesque and actor Jean Duceppe, then president of the performers' union, l'Union des artistes.[9]

These two well-known figures, important players in this labour conflict, got involved in mounting a major production called *Difficultés temporaires* (*Temporary Difficulties*) as a show of solidarity with the striking producers. Jean Duceppe and a fellow actor, Jean-Louis Roux[10] (later head of the Canada Council for the Arts), had mobilized Quebec's entire artistic community to support the striking producers. Those who had become television stars over the last few years leapt to the barricades beside the producers. Not surprisingly, the population ended up choosing sides; they rallied around the strikers — and their stars! The return to work was enthusiastic, the producers having won the union accreditation they were seeking. They were also convinced that they had contributed to the cultural fulfillment of their fellow francophones.

Why did the government let the strike go on for so long? It was probably in part because it could not stand the idea that the French network would have a different union structure than the English network. But it is also clear that senior management at Radio-Canada were afraid to leave too much decision-making power in the hands of the producers.

Historically, majority governments tend to be arrogant towards CBC/Radio-Canada. It was true under John Diefenbaker's Conservative government in 1959, just a few months after his party won a crushing majority, and it has been true in other eras as well.

Another telling incident, which happened at the English network in 1959, left its mark among CBC staff in Toronto. CBC's managing director, Ernie Bushnell, ordered the cancellation of the short daily morning radio program, *Preview Commentary*. The program was said to displease Prime Minister Diefenbaker because its commentaries were often critical of his government. The decision to cancel the program had been accepted by the entire senior management team, but some thirty producers drew a line in the sand, threatening to resign immediately. The president, Alphonse Ouimet, and the board were forced to stand down. Everyone was convinced that the order to cancel the program had come straight from the minister responsible for the CBC, George Nowlan, but Ernie Bushnell always denied it.

The End of the Duplessis Era

Meanwhile, in Quebec, Premier Maurice Duplessis, obsessed with his hatred of communism, observed all this while grumbling. He believed Radio-Canada television had become a nest of opposition to his political power. But was this really the case?

In a program on the occasion of Radio-Canada's fiftieth anniversary in 1986, René Lévesque said that television had served as a kind of indicator of what was going on throughout society. In the same program, Gérard Pelletier[11] recognized that Radio-Canada had "certainly contributed to lifting restrictions and allowing societal debates."[12] We are talking here about a time when the dominant axis of discussion was the opposition between progressive and conservative ideas. It was also a time when those who formed the progressive francophone opposition were not yet tearing each other apart over federalism and Quebec independence.

Maurice Duplessis died a few months after the end of the producers' strike. A new wind was blowing across Quebec. I have a childhood memory of seeing thousands of people filing by the coffin of the man who had exercised such iron control over Quebec.

"The premier of Quebec has died," my father told me in a solemn tone. Even though he was a Liberal, he respected the office of premier. Then, sitting in our living room, we watched the long funeral procession from Trois-Rivières. The program was impressive for a six-year-old child.

For the first time, Radio-Canada deployed its big arsenal of cameras for a major event. This first major special was produced by the Religious Programs section of Radio-Canada, not the News Service. This may have been understandable in 1959, but thinking of it now I remember the malaise among Radio-Canada's journalists in September 1984, when the responsibility for coverage of John Paul II's papal visit to Canada was handed to the same Religious Programs section ... the old debate on the separation of Church and State....

Be that as it may, with Duplessis's death, we felt that something new was about to happen — or at least, that is what our parents said. After that, television introduced us to an entirely new figure: the incoming premier, Paul Sauvé. History would credit him with many accomplishments in a short time — just 114 days in power. For my part, the only child-hood memory I retain about Premier Paul Sauvé is that his death was announced by Jacques Fauteux on the Radio-Canada newscast of January 2, 1960. These developments grabbed all the attention of the guests at our family holiday dinner in the country. The party took on an undesirable atmosphere for a seven-year-old child. We had to learn the name of a third premier, Antonio Barrette, in a few months.

Lesage and Lévesque in Power

This premier's name was also a flash in the pan. A new name was on everyone's lips — Jean Lesage. He took power in June 1960 with his *équipe du tonnerre* (spectacular team), which included the established television star René Lévesque. A true revolution ... but quiet, even at home, where my parents were delighted with this political change!

For Radio-Canada, this was a first. One of its own star personal-ities was in power. It was also a first for the journalists in the newsroom, who had to cover the actions and the political speeches of one of their own. It would not be the last time; the same scenario would unfold over subsequent years, for example when Gérard Pelletier and Jeanne Sauvé also jumped into the political arena. There is nothing new about pol-itical parties calling on good communicators with high profiles to join their ranks. It is easy to understand, especially when you see how fluidly someone like René Lévesque could answer reporters' questions and how superbly he performed on shows such as *Les Couche-tard*.

At the time, René Lévesque was in the Liberal party, which formed a single organization in Ottawa and in Quebec City. The Quebec Liberal Party was not, as it is today, a free-standing organization, independent from the Liberal Party of Canada. There was no need to feel out of step when Lévesque and Lesage were re-elected in 1962 and Liberal Lester B. Pearson was elected in Ottawa in 1963. The only difference was that Pearson headed a minority government after years of majority Conservative government under John Diefenbaker — the same Diefenbaker who had been so hostile to the awakening of francophones through the magic box of Radio-Canada.

We had the impression — or at least that is what my parents told me, and I still believed them at the time — that everything was going well.

The Collision of Nationalisms

However, a great schism was brewing in the French-Canadian community, an epic battle between two forms of nationalism: French-Canadian nationalism on one side and the new Quebec nationalism on the other. The two sides would be led by two established Radio-Canada stars: first and foremost, René Lévesque, but also a certain Pierre Trudeau, co-founder with Gérard Pelletier of *Cité libre* magazine, who had been a high-profile guest on many Radio-Canada current affairs shows. Furthermore, there were several streams forming within the Quebec nationalist movement itself. This came to everyone's attention quite violently in March 1963, when the first bomb planted by the Front de libération du Québec exploded in Montreal. The mounting struggles to find the right strategy for the fulfillment of Quebec were becoming increasingly obvious.

Radio-Canada was subjected to these pressures — and sometimes to the wrath of the federal government, whether the government in power in Ottawa was Liberal or Conservative. Meanwhile, following the division of the French Canadian nation into two adversarial camps, it suddenly became necessary to redefine their respective ideologies. On one hand, there was a Canadian vision of the future of French Canadians, on the other, a Québécois vision of the future of franco-phones. French Canadians outside Quebec, abandoned in this process, had to find their own way. In this new landscape, Radio-Canada's jour-nalists were determined to practise a high quality of journalism. From now on, Radio-Canada's radio and television networks would have to deal with the different political vantage points in Quebec society. Welcome to the new era!

CHAPTER 3

The End of the Monopoly, the Beginning of Tensions

February 9, 1961, was the launch date for Télé-Métropole, Quebec's brand new private television station. Radio-Canada's exclusive access to the population was over!

The shock was brutal. Up to that point, everyone had watched the only available programming. Now that there was competition, the public had a choice.

With the arrival of this competitor, which soon overshadowed the established station, Radio-Canada could have defined a new personality for itself. From the fall of 1952 until the winter of 1961, especially in the Montreal area, Radio-Canada had had a monopoly on creative expression and was alone in taking advantage of the popularity that came with that. The public broadcaster even seemed to see itself as the sole proprietor of the airwaves for all time. The arrival of Télé-Métropole, Channel 10, brought with it a serious lesson in humility.

With famous and popular stars like Olivier Guimond, among others, Télé-Métropole's future — and its creativity — was guaranteed. From 1962 on, the children's show *Capitaine Bonhomme*[1] reached a wide audience with originality and verve, even if some parents found the program a little vulgar for their children's chaste little ears, more used to the gentler *La Boîte à surprises*[2] and *Fanfreluche*.[3]

At the opening of the second television network in 1961, Jean Lesage declared, "We are confident that Télé-Métropole will serve the interests of French Canada."[4] The challenge of faithfully representing francophones on television had been launched by the premier of Quebec himself.

And yet, Radio-Canada had been useful to the Quebec Liberal Party by providing a platform for opposition voices during the rule of Maurice Duplessis. Some people went so far as to say that the true Ministry of Culture in Quebec was Radio-Canada.

The New Normal

After having absorbed the shock of the arrival of its first competitor, Radio-Canada television devoted itself to attempting to regain its lost popularity. But was there a real, in-depth examination? Acknowledging the appearance of a competitor is one thing, but defining a new mission for the new circumstances is quite another. This was to become even more problematic since, from the time of the launch of Télé-Métropole, the hybrid financing formula — government subsidies plus commercial revenues — began to create enormous pressures on the public service orientation. Those in charge of programming had to create a schedule that clearly differentiated the public from the private broadcaster, and this was obviously a major challenge.

In reality, no one understood the importance of these new circum-stances at the time — although some may have preferred to ignore them. There was never a true debate on defining the new conditions among elected officials or inside Radio-Canada, and certainly not within Quebec society. So Radio-Canada muddled along, trying to find the right balance between its public service mandate and the need to find commercial rev-enues, just like its private competitor, in order to assemble resources for its operating budget. The public broadcaster often did this imaginatively and successfully; at other times it deviated significantly from its man-date, sometimes by inappropriately copying its competitor. The methods could differ substantially under the different management in charge at any given time.

This was a botched opportunity, since the hybrid financing model was too rigid and has always been a burden. It would have been worthwhile at the time to research models invented in other countries, for example the direct licence fees paid by owners of television sets in the United Kingdom. This kind of independent public financing has the advantage of being stable and far less vulnerable to the political climate of the day.

By contrast, the Canadian financing model has long linked the public broadcaster to the government and placed it squarely at the mercy of politicians. In order to top up its budget, Radio-Canada had no other choice: it had to fall back on commercial revenues. From now on, it would have to cope with economic volatility and the search for audiences.

This perpetual uncertainty influenced the kind of programming on offer. It opened up Radio-Canada to criticism for offering overly mass-market or popular programming, or for competing "unfairly" with the private sector.

"What is the point of a public information service that does things just like its private competitors?" I believe that this question, which I asked employees in my 2012 goodbye letter to them,[5] is the essential question, which Radio-Canada has never truly answered.[6] Since the launch of their first private sector competitor in 1961, the dilemma has haunted public television, which has never been able to reconcile the two opposing visions. Become PBS North?[7] Never! Radio-Canada must not be elitist and must serve all citizens! It is possible to be popular without being elitist! There is no public service without the public! These are some of the statements that we have heard on the subject over the last forty years. Throughout this time, Radio-Canada has been pushed around according to the vagaries of the government of the day. When the government cuts off its funding, Radio-Canada tries to compensate by seeking commercial revenues at all costs. As we will see, this situation has created fragility in the public service today, at a time when public support is at its lowest because of the digital disruption.

Already in 1966, after just five years of coexistence between Télé-Métropole and Radio-Canada, journalist André Laurendeau was warning Radio-Canada against the temptation to imitate its competitor:

> Radio-Canada must adapt to the competition and often does this badly.... It seems to me that the French network [Radio-Canada] is trying to bring back its audience

by using the same tools as its main Montreal rival…. I believe this is a mistake.[8]

The Great Divide Among Francophones

The very same André Laurendeau co-chaired the Royal Commission on Bilingualism and Biculturalism (B&B),[9] which tried to find answers to the question of what place francophones should have in this country. The problem was urgent because of increasingly vocal dissatisfaction in Quebec every time some injustice appeared on the horizon. Radio-Canada was the place for these discussions. However, the multiple chapters of the B&B Commission report were shelved and forgotten. At the same time, the great divide between Quebec francophones and those in the other provinces became painfully obvious in the course of a series of meetings organized by *L'Action nationale* magazine, with the collaboration of several other organizations, such as the Saint-Jean-Baptiste Society. These encounters, dubbed the Estates General of French Canada, culminated in a large gathering in the Salle Wilfrid-Pelletier in Montreal's Place-des-Arts, bringing together fifteen hundred people, three hundred of them from other provinces. Jacques-Yvan Morin, a university professor and future Parti Québécois cabinet minister, chaired the event. Journalists such as Jean-Marc Léger, who would later become an *indépendantiste*, and future senator Solange Chaput-Rolland, who would come to choose federalism, were active participants.

Those who were partisans of Quebec nationalism dominated those who were French-Canadian nationalists. Their interpretation of the history of French Canada swept away the traditional one, considered old-fashioned by the new Quebec nationalists. The Franco-Ontarians and Acadians came away from this exercise bloodied and bruised, with the impression of having been judged as the guardians of a vision of the common history of francophones that was mired in the past and now irrelevant. The Quebec nationalists seemed to be on the side of a strong future Quebec that would be the only state capable of ensuring that francophones could flourish culturally. They might be a minority within Canada, but they were now a majority within Quebec! The gulf between the two visions was so wide that some Franco-Ontarians whom I knew well chose precisely that time, coming out of the Estates General of French Canada, to move permanently to Quebec. This new state of affairs provoked many struggles within the management of the French-language Radio-Canada, particularly because it was becoming increasingly difficult to provide common programming that could satisfy both Quebec francophones and the ones who lived elsewhere in Canada.

At the same time, young students such as my classmates and I found that we all had to redefine ourselves. Who were we now? Were we Québécois, French Canadians, Canadians? Our questioning almost foreshadowed the famous scene in the comedy film *Elvis Gratton*, with its uproariously funny eponymous character,[10] created by writer and filmmaker Pierre Falardeau. The new search for identity among Quebec francophones was well and truly launched.

The 1960s

At the beginning of the 1960s, new political ideas began to take shape in Quebec.

Bearing witness to these changes, Radio-Canada opened up its airwaves to debates. There were several different proposals: there was the idea of special status touted by Paul Gérin-Lajoie; the full independence of Quebec, the position of the Rassemblement pour l'indépendance nationale (RIN) led by Pierre Bourgault; sovereignty-association, proposed by René Lévesque; the two nations theory, supported by several federalists; as well as the "equal or independent" position of Daniel Johnson. And, of course, the more radical action approach of the FLQ, which also had supporters.

Daniel Johnson Sr. was the person who best described the dilemma that would haunt the debate for many years to come:

> There remain only two possible options between which we will have to choose before 1967: either we will be masters of our own destiny in Quebec and equal partners in the management of the country, or we will be completely separate.[11]

This, of course, did not foresee the vision of Pierre Elliott Trudeau. The scene was set for more than a decade, far beyond 1967....

The 1960s were also years of confrontation and labour demands. They saw the emancipation of women and the advent of the birth control pill, which upset sexual habits, as well as the exodus of the faithful from the Catholic church. Culturally, we celebrated the Beatles' visit to Montreal just as much as the spectacular explosion of Quebec songs and culture. We sang our pride during Expo 67, an incomparable place for culture, debates, and discovery. Everything was interrelated; it was a great cry of the heart for a society exploding with ideas expressing its immense desire for liberation. These events and new ideas were abundantly reflected by Radio-Canada. In that sense, the archives of the public broadcaster constitute an exceptional national heritage.

Tremors in Ottawa

The debates on the future of Quebec in Canada occupied a huge place in the public consciousness of the decade. No wonder! The option favouring the outright separation of Quebec had already arrived on the scene with the creation of Pierre Bourgault's RIN. This option was gaining in popularity, first with the creation of René Lévesque's Mouvement souveraineté-association, then with the birth of the Parti Québécois in 1968.

This was the moment when the political powers in Ottawa began seeking a way of avoiding the full-frontal collision that was looming on the horizon. In 1965, the prime minister of Canada, Lester B. Pearson, had recruited not one but three new personalities. The three future ministers known as *les trois colombes* ("the three doves") were Jean Marchand, Gérard Pelletier, and Pierre Trudeau. Of the three, Trudeau was the one who most forcefully proposed a more structured vision of the country. A larger-than-life public intellectual with a modern style, he was the incarnation of the renewal that many people sought — except that his ideas quickly clashed with an entirely different vision of the country.

Even before the energetic rise of René Lévesque's option, in the period when Pierre Trudeau was a Liberal minister in Ottawa (1967–1968)[12] he began to denounce the Quebec nationalist vision, whether it was that of Liberal Jean Lesage or that of Daniel Johnson, the Union Nationale premier. Before entering politics, Trudeau had frequently appeared on programs where ideas were debated on Radio-Canada television. Over the years he had defended an idea of the future of French Canadians that was diametrically opposed to the one proposed by the *séparatistes*[13] led by Pierre Bourgault and, primarily, René Lévesque. A battle of titans was set between René Lévesque and Pierre Trudeau.

It was not surprising that Trudeau was so critical of Radio-Canada the minute the public television network reflected ideas opposed to his own about the future of francophones. Radio-Canada's independence from the federal government would be brutally challenged. Trudeau had long made known his intentions with regard to the role of federal government institutions. In 1967, he had clearly set out his thinking in his book *Le Fédéralisme et la société canadienne-française.*

In the book, he had laid out precisely the role that certain federal institutions should play in the area of ideas and culture, in order to counter separatist ideas:

> One of the ways to counter the attraction of separatism is to allocate time, energy and large sums of money to serve federal nationalism. The idea is to create an image of the national reality so attractive that it makes that of the separatist group uninteresting in comparison. We need to allocate some resources to things like the flag, the national anthem, education, arts councils, radio and television broadcasters and film boards.[14]

Allocating "large sums of money to serve federal nationalism [and] resources to things ... like radio and television broadcasters." You'd have to be naive not to read political intent into this statement and even perhaps a foreshadowing of the real struggle that would unfold in the following years between federalists and separatists, including on the airwaves at Radio-Canada, stuck between a rock and a hard place.

On Monday, July 24, 1967, these tensions were all exacerbated by a surprising speech given by General Charles de Gaulle from the balcony of

Montreal City Hall. "Vive le Québec libre!" ("Long live a free Quebec!") the president of France called out to the partisans of independence, who rejoiced at this unexpected manna from heaven. For the first time, their struggle was being endorsed by a person of historical stature. One of my brothers, born on July 24, found that those around the table were taking little interest in his birthday celebration that night. Charles de Gaulle, a celebrity intruder, had stolen his thunder. De Gaulle's shocking declaration was the only subject of conversation. Two days later, on July 26, our family viewed the response from Mayor Jean Drapeau at the good-bye dinner for the general. This led to new discussions. Was De Gaulle a hero? Had he been wrong to say those famous words? Had Drapeau been rude to give De Gaulle a history lesson about France's abandonment of Canada's francophones in 1763? We were all a bit taken aback by the things we were seeing on Radio-Canada. We understood that for our family, the debate on the future of Quebec had just become the elephant in the room.

A year later, Pierre Trudeau, who had been elected leader of the Liberal Party after Prime Minister Pearson stepped down, showed up on a famous June 24 among the dignitaries on the raised platform to watch the Saint-Jean-Baptiste Day parade. A series of traditional and largely insignificant floats passed the platform uneventfully, but a bit further, a group of separatist demonstrators had gathered. Defiantly, the new leader of the Liberal Party remained on the platform as they launched various projectiles at him. The demonstrators were also helping to launch his political career! The next day, in the election of June 25, 1968, he harvested many more votes than he had hoped. The newspaper headlines trumpeted, "Trudeau Wins" and "Trudeau's Victory."

Unfortunately, Radio-Canada was not able to fulfil its role by providing live coverage of Trudeau's victory on that night. Did we have public radio and television or state radio and television? Let's go back for a moment to that parade on June 24, 1968. While the cameras assigned to Radio-Canada's live special ignored what was going on outside the perimeter defined by the Saint-Jean-Baptiste parade organizers, another parade was forming just a few metres away. The demonstrators, among them Pierre Bourgault, leader of the RIN, were protesting the good-natured, childlike celebration of the old-fashioned holiday. Just a few years later, the day would be declared Quebec's national holiday (Fête nationale du Québec), although west of Quebec it remains to this day the religious holiday to mark the birth of St. John the Baptist, the patron saint of French Canadians.[15] The violent confrontation between the demonstrators and the police on June 24, 1968, is also part of the history of Quebec and of Radio-Canada.

One of Radio-Canada's television reporters, Claude Jean Devirieux, wanted to describe the events exactly as he had seen them. He even cited on air the badge number of a particularly aggressive police officer. He was swiftly disciplined. The next morning, Radio-Canada management immediately suspended him. His colleagues then walked off the job. In his 2012 book, Devirieux wrote,

> My bosses, terrified by the calls to protest, suspended me for the day, with pay. My colleagues at work, all the reporters who had covered the election campaign, refused to work without me, saying that they could not provide complete and credible coverage without my participation. The technicians followed suit. For the first time since the creation of Radio-Canada in 1952, there was no election evening special (*La soirée des elections*) — on the very day that was to be the electoral triumph of Pierre Elliott Trudeau. He never forgot it.[16]

Indeed, there is no trace of the federal election special of June 25, 1968, in Radio-Canada's archives. This confrontation marked the beginning of a period of acute tension between the majority Liberal government and Radio-Canada.

In an interview for this book, Devirieux remained convinced that the events of June 24, 1968, tarnished the rest of his career and blocked his professional advancement.

At my home that night, there was a vigorous inter-generational discussion. After all, said my parents, wasn't Pierre Trudeau one of our own? How could we inflict such an insult on him when a French Canadian would be leading Canada? Yes, but his French-Canadian nationalism may not be the same as ours, we are Québécois, we dared to add to the discussion. The political allegiances of young francophones were being redefined at lightning speed!

Already, a few months before that memorable Saint-Jean-Baptiste Day, on March 7, 1968, the Liberal government of Lester B. Pearson had adopted new legislation redefining Radio-Canada's mission. The new law stipulated in English that CBC/Radio-Canada was to "contribute to the development of national unity and provide for a continuing expression of Canadian identity" and was translated in French as "contribuer au développement de l'unité nationale et d'exprimer constamment la réalité canadienne."[17] This definition would satisfy the complaints of those who were always accusing Radio-Canada of being a hive of separatists.

Barely one month later, on April 7, Pierre Trudeau would become the leader of the Liberal Party of Canada, then prime minister on April 20. At the time of the bill's passage, he was minister of justice and therefore not responsible for CBC/Radio-Canada. No doubt his influence on the party was already considerable, and in the light of his previous statements, he would have been completely onside with the legislation.

On another front, CBC/Radio-Canada requested statutory financing for a period of five years. This was refused. The public broadcaster had to resign itself to annual government decisions to maintain, increase, or reduce its budget. This state of affairs, which continues to this day, has always made planning very difficult at Radio-Canada and forces it to beg the government for money every year. Clearly, this is a state of dependence.

Finally, the new Broadcasting Act specified that CBC/Radio-Canada would now be subject to the jurisdiction of the CRTC, which had become the regulatory agency in charge of evaluating whether or not the organization was fulfilling its mandate properly.

Benoît Lévesque and Jean-Guy Lacroix, professors in the department of sociology at UQAM, wrote in 1988,

> Once entirely under the jurisdiction of the CRTC, SRC's powers were reduced, especially since it had not succeeded in obtaining the five-year statutory financing

that it considered important for its autonomy. The specific provision in its mandate to contribute to Canadian national unity was a particularly difficult challenge for the French-language networks at a time when the Quebec nationalist movement was in full swing.[18]

Radio-Canada, then, was under surveillance, and did not always enjoy the necessary freedom to fully play its role as an independent public service. Under such circumstances, it is very difficult to enforce the idea of arm's length.

In the meantime, an important development took place in July 1968: Raymond David became vice-president and general manager of the French-language services of CBC/Radio-Canada and affirmed the autonomy of the French services within the Crown corporation.

Nearly ten years had gone by since the producers' strike, and francophones were increasingly present in senior management. Raymond David was very representative of Quebec's Quiet Revolution. One of a large family from working-class Rosemont, he had studied at Collège Sainte-Marie and taught at the elite Collège Jean-de-Brébeuf before becoming director of Radio-Collège in the mid-1950s. He had then gone to Paris and London to pursue his studies in political science. He was well acquainted with the young politicians who would later play such major roles in our history, such as Pierre Trudeau, René Lévesque, Robert Bourassa, and Pierre Bourgault. From the 1950s until his departure from Radio-Canada in 1982, he shaped the institution. At a very young age, at the time of Radio-Collège, he had made friends with the young producer Marc Thibault, another person who would come to play an important role in the future.

Marc Thibault had also come to know several politicians while producing public affairs shows, notably with René Lévesque and Gérard Pelletier. He had overseen such programs from the beginning of the 1960s until 1982. The David-Thibault team was at the very top of Radio-Canada when Pierre Trudeau became prime minister in 1968, during the October Crisis of 1970, at the time of the election of the Parti Québécois in 1976, and during the first Quebec referendum in 1980. These two lived through tumultuous times. At the time, it was common to poke fun at the situation by saying that Radio-Canada was run by Jesuits. It was true that both men were erudite, that they wrote in impeccable French, and that they attached great importance to intellectual rigour, sometimes down to the smallest detail. The younger journalists found Marc Thibault forbidding and authoritarian, perhaps even a bit haughty; this is why he was sometimes nicknamed God the Father.

The "Key in the Mailbox"

A few months after his election, with a big majority government under his belt, Prime Minister Pierre Trudeau indulged himself on several occasions by reprimanding Radio-Canada. This reached a climax on October 19, 1969, when he proclaimed in front of four thousand Liberal party supporters: "The fooling around is over!" He accused Radio-Canada of favouring the cause of sovereignty, and even threatened to "put the key in the mailbox"![19]

The next day, Trudeau spoke in a similar vein in a famous interview with host Louis Martin and journalist Gérard Gravel on a public affairs show called *Format 30*:

> "People are fed up with a certain lack of objectivity among the journalists at Radio-Canada who seem to favour the separatists and only cover debates involving separatists …. Is there any room left in the news for anything else but separatism?"
>
> "People are wondering," said Louis Martin, "if Radio-Canada could be put into trusteeship."
>
> "It's possible," retorted Pierre Trudeau without hesitation.
>
> "In the near future?" asked Martin.
>
> "If we see that the taxpayer's dollar is not properly spent at Radio-Canada, we will not hesitate to chop the budget as we have done [at the Ministry of Defence]."[20]

The tone had been set. Radio-Canada and its journalists were on notice about the Trudeau era.

The following day, October 21, Louis Martin, true to himself, looked for balance. This time, it was René Lévesque's turn to counterattack. He suspected Radio-Canada's management of having obeyed the Trudeau government's orders to end the systematic coverage of political party conventions. The decision had been made immediately before the Parti Québécois convention that was set to begin on October 17, 1969.[21]

In his book on the history of radio, Pierre Pagé says that in the following days, Claude Ryan wrote the first of a series of three editorials in *Le Devoir*: "The Malaise at Radio-Canada"; "The Temperamental Anger of the Prince: Where do the problems that so exasperate Mr. Trudeau come from?"; and "Are the Real Problems the Ones Mr. Trudeau sees?"

Ryan wrote,

> A long tradition confirmed by the 1968 Broadcasting Act directs that in Canada, the public broadcaster be established on a footing that guarantees its independence from political power. Neither Mr. Saint-Laurent, nor Mr. Diefenbaker, nor Mr. Pearson[22] were able to take the liberty of diverging from this discipline.[23]

The journalists and management of Radio-Canada were very aware that things would never again be simple. How could they report on the fundamental debate that was taking place in Quebec society when the federal political power was so hostile and, more importantly, held the purse strings?

One soothing balm on the wounds incurred in these exchanges: Gérard Pelletier, then secretary of state, dissociated himself a few days later from the attacks his leader, Pierre Trudeau, had inflicted on Radio-Canada. On October 25, in a speech entitled "Why Radio-Canada Was Created Free," he reminded everyone that the institution reported to the Canadian Parliament as a whole, and that it must establish its independence from political power.[24]

For his part, Radio-Canada's vice-president, Raymond David,

passionately defended the independence of the public service: "It is a great disservice to Radio-Canada to be, in spite of itself, at the centre of the crisis which is being felt across all of French Canada."[25] Indeed, it was not easy to reflect all the differences when some would prefer to ignore the main public debate under way at the time.

Be that as it may, the harm was done. Such an explosive climate was bad for the freedom and independence of the Information Service (News and Current Affairs) and for the whole institution. For a few years afterwards, journalists were always guarded and felt that they were under constant surveillance. Should they exercise self-censorship? Not go too far in order to avoid being penalized professionally or worsening the situation at Radio-Canada? Obviously, these questions were being asked. They even provoked debates because some felt that it was vital to affirm the independence of the news and to deal with all subjects in complete freedom and without any form of censorship or hindrance. Others felt that the working climate had been poisoned.

This is what happens when governments put pressure on the public broadcaster, particularly with regard to television, the most important mass medium of its time. No doubt the Liberal majority justified such arrogance — and besides, this was the essential struggle of Pierre Trudeau's life. The excellent host and journalist Louis Martin, fed up with this climate, left Radio-Canada in 1971 to teach journalism at Laval University and to run the French-language edition of *Maclean's* magazine (subsequently *L'actualité*.) After four years there, he returned to Radio-Canada in a management position; he later returned once again to an on-air role hosting shows. In the 1990s, he went back into management as head of Radio News and Current Affairs.

Just as John Diefenbaker's Conservative government had done during the producers' strike ten years earlier, Trudeau could afford to remind Radio-Canada who was in charge.

Conservatives or Liberals — it was still same fight against the independence of the public broadcaster.

Radio-Canada hadn't seen anything yet. The October Crisis exploded in the fall of 1970.

CHAPTER 4

A Collision of Identities:
From the October Crisis in 1970 to the Election of the Parti Québécois in 1976

In the fall of 1990, I produced a report on the October Crisis and the media for the public affairs program *Le Point*. Marc Thibault, who had headed up Radio-Canada's News and Information Services from 1968 to 1981, talked about the tumultuous years of his mandate. I was privileged to have several exchanges with him on the subject.

Marc Thibault was one of the most iconic figures of Radio-Canada's history. He was the one in charge when Pierre Trudeau threatened to "put the key in the mailbox." In fact, he was probably the most ardent defender of the independence of Radio-Canada's News and Current Affairs Service in the face of pressure from politicians and lobbies of all stripes. He was an inspiration for many journalists and managers in his time and in the following generations, of which I was a member. During the 1970s, Thibault had to defend his organization several times in front of the Parliamentary Commission in Ottawa, at the CRTC, and on other platforms.

Above all, what he sought to protect was Radio-Canada's indispensable independence at arm's length from political power. For him, Radio-Canada's radio and television services were above all public institutions, and therefore not meant to be subservient to the state or the government of the day but rather to serve the public at large. There must always exist a Great Wall between Radio-Canada and those in political power, even if the government of the day granted its annual budget.

Through his vision, Thibault made an inestimable contribution to the building of a strong journalistic culture at Radio-Canada, which continues to inspire the artisans of today's public service broadcaster. In an internal memo on March 10, 1977, Thibault wrote:

> As a public service broadcaster, Radio-Canada can in no way, shape or form be used as an instrument for propaganda, no matter on whose behalf. We are first and foremost a press enterprise and we must assume the imperatives of free information.[1]

The October Crisis

One of the most important political crises in this country's history exploded onto the scene on October 5, 1970. It all began with the kidnapping of a British diplomat, James Richard Cross, by the FLQ. Then a provincial cabinet minister, Pierre Laporte, was kidnapped on October 10, held, and assassinated by FLQ members. His body was found in the trunk of a car on October 17, the day after the implementation of the War Measures Act. There had never been a similar situation in peacetime Canada. From the beginning of the October Crisis, the FLQ cells were using the media, particularly certain private radio stations (CKAC and CKLM), to broadcast their releases.

With the passage of the War Measures Act, all were subjected to censorship. In a report broadcast twenty years later, Marc Thibault remembered,

> I think that Radio-Canada did a substantial job of covering the crisis, and of analysing it as well. Not the way the privates did it, and for good reason. Think of CKAC, which for all intents and purposes, controlled the transmission of releases from the FLQ, until censorship was enforced and forbade the broadcast of the FLQ releases unless it was authorised by the police.[2]

At Radio-Canada, the situation was even more complex, as Thibault acknowledged in an interview with journalist Claude Sauvé.

Thibault: I think that Radio-Canada evolved during the crisis with more, let's call it "moderation."

Sauvé: Because you encouraged Radio-Canada staff to demonstrate moderation?

Thibault: Because there was the reality that, precisely, an effort to interpret the War Measures Act, an effort to interpret that, had perhaps been pushed at Radio-Canada, and for good reason. Because Radio-Canada, as a public enterprise, was equipped with a legal service that could judge the interpretation of the law. A legal service whose staff spread out to the studios so that certain Radio-Canada journalists had the feeling that their work was being done subject to legal or judicial control.[3]

This was indeed a unique situation, one that deeply worried the journalists at Radio-Canada.

In October 1970, they were not the only ones to worry about censorship and the impact of the War Measures Act on their work. On October 17, the editor-in-chief of *Le Devoir*, Claude Ryan, sounded the alarm in an editorial:

This law confers such vast powers on the central government that it had never, in living history, been invoked in peacetime. It is the first time in the entire history of Confederation that a government dares to invoke such an extreme law to maintain internal peace.[4]

Ryan's interventions, and his connections with other personalities, including René Lévesque, caused him to be accused of plotting a *coup d'état* in Quebec. Peter C. Newman took up the accusation in the *Toronto Star*, insisting that he had heard the information from a "very high level source" in Ottawa.

For Radio-Canada, the crisis was unprecedented. Radio-Canada's arm's-length relationship with political power, its so-called Great Wall, was gravely threatened by the War Measures Act and the warmongering discourse that accompanied it.

The death of Pierre Laporte put an abrupt end to any sympathy the FLQ had previously enjoyed among the Quebec population. Up until then, whether it was openly acknowledged or not, everyone had been talking about the crisis. For many, the FLQ's actions were first perceived as the defiant rebuke of young idealists against the overly established powers that be.

Some had actually revelled in Gaétan Montreuil's reading of the FLQ manifesto on Radio-Canada television. But Pierre Laporte's assassination was too much. At home, parents and children had no sympathy for this at all. For once, there was a rare convergence of opinion between occasionally saucy young people and their elders; we all said at once, "It just isn't done, to kill somebody!"

Reflections or Propaganda

After the October Crisis, far from subsiding, the tensions within Quebec society and the confrontations between federalists and sovereigntists grew in intensity. At Radio-Canada, the News and Current Affairs Service had a mandate to reflect the range of popular opinion on the subject. Here, public service took on its true meaning: the role of journalists was to bear witness without taking part in the debates and issues unfolding before them. They took this role seriously despite the challenges, while Ottawa continued to see things quite differently. There were constant reminders of the famous mission defined in the 1968 Broadcasting Act, which imposed on Radio-Canada the obligation to "contribute to the development of national unity and provide for a continuing expression of Canadian identity."[5]

Marc Raboy reports in his book that during the debate in the House of Commons when the Act was adopted, the discussion of the meaning of the expression "national unity" had provoked a reaction from Gérard Pelletier, who was uneasy with the definition, since "it could lead some to believe that it meant not promotion, but propaganda."[6]

The 1968 Act created a malaise in Radio-Canada's management, which is evident in several documents of the time. Draft programming policies from 1971 show attempts to figure out how to interpret this mandate. The 1982 edition of the Journalism Policy says: "The Parliament of Canada, through the 1968 Broadcasting Act, imposed[7] on CBC/Radio-Canada the obligation to 'contribute to the development of national unity and to provide for a continuing expression of Canadian identity.'" (In French, the reference was to a continuing expression of Canadian reality.)

This policy refers several times to Radio-Canada's attachment to its objectivity, but one paragraph on current affairs programs is an example of a contradiction:

> Public affairs programs must reflect Canada as a nation and invoke the social, economic, cultural and political **advantages** each one of us gains from belonging to the Canadian community. However, public affairs programs must also depict the tensions within this society and describe the proposed changes in political and constitutional structure with a view to reducing these tensions and to make known the **cost** and the **consequences** of these changes.[8]

This was a real puzzle for all the journalists who had to figure out how to deal with this definition of Radio-Canada's mandate and yet still profess at the same time their impartiality, neutrality, and journalistic independence. All this at the same time as Quebec society was becoming radically polarized between federalists and sovereigntists, between the opposing camps of Canada's prime minister, Pierre Trudeau, and that of the leader of the Parti Québécois, René Lévesque.

The new prime minister of Canada wanted to push the further Canadianization of the cultural and communications sector, first to oppose American continental cultural domination, but also to put forward his concept of federal nationalism and to fight Quebec nationalism fiercely.

In order to accomplish this, a few months after his election to the country's highest political office in June 1968 he reconfigured the structure of his cabinet, creating a cabinet committee on culture and information to be led by the secretary of state, the predecessor to the Ministry of Communications (later the Ministry of Canadian Heritage). Radio-Canada would come under the jurisdiction of the secretary of state.

It is obvious that under these circumstances, Radio-Canada was under surveillance. A few years later, the Liberals went even further, proposing Bill C-24, the intent of which was to exercise closer control over Crown corporations, including Radio-Canada:

> [The law] aimed to control development plans and operational budgets of Crown Corporations, to impose political directives, to control them through laws and the ability to disavow. Several senior cabinet ministers, including Jean Chrétien, insisted that this law should apply to the Canada Council, the National Arts Centre, the Canadian Film Development Corporation (CFDC) and to Radio-Canada; this failed primarily because of the storm of protests ... which greeted this proposal.[9]

The immense collision of identities within Quebec can be traced to this moment.

The Shock of the Election of the Parti Québécois

On November 15, 1976, Radio-Canada covered the Quebec election results live to air. The audience for the public broadcaster's special program included the vast majority of francophone viewers. At the time, Télé-Métropole just wasn't up to speed in the area of live election coverage.

All of Quebec was watching when news anchor Bernard Derome announced, "Radio-Canada, at 8:40 p.m., predicts that the next government of Quebec will be formed by the Parti Québécois and that it will be a majority government." This announcement was immediately followed by enthusiastic applause from some members of the studio audience. Despite repeated explanations by Radio-Canada management about the live audience in studio, some people persisted in believing (somewhat obsessively) that the applause had come from the public broadcaster's journalists.

The election of the Parti Québécois launched a true shock wave in Ottawa. It was an election victory for René Lévesque, but a personal defeat for Pierre Trudeau. The response would be sharp and bitter. It was too much!

Radio-Canada's journalists were accused of having favoured the election of René Lévesque's party. A witch hunt for sovereigntist journalists was launched. The head of News and Current Affairs, Marc Thibault, defended his people tooth and nail against accusations from the party in power in Ottawa.

The Quebec caucus of the federal Liberal party reproached Radio-Canada with not having promoted national unity. The same MPs concluded that their suspicions were well-founded when a handful of Radio-Canada journalists resigned and moved from Montreal to Quebec City to become political staffers in the new PQ government. As Thibault confided in me in 1990, the perception created in political circles and in the population by these resignations made his job as senior executive in charge of news and public programming at Radio-Canada even more difficult.

On the political scene, the Quebec nationalism expressed in the 1976 election was distinctly different from the traditional French-Canadian nationalism, which retained a strong sense of belonging to Canada. Now each side identified with its respective territory. Quebec or Canada? The Government of Canada's first disciplinary interventions at Radio-Canada were provoked by this collision of identities among the various francophone groups across the country. Should Radio-Canada's French-language services serve the population of Canada or the population of Quebec, which had just elected a sovereigntist government?

On March 4, 1977, a few months after the election of the Parti Québécois, Pierre Trudeau wrote to the chair of the CRTC, Harry Boyle, successor to Pierre Juneau, to ask him to investigate whether "the French and English-language networks of SRC fulfilled their mandate in general, and particularly in their public affairs and news programs." He added, "Given the gravity of the issue, you will agree with me that it is imperative to have a report in hand between now and July 1."[10]

The CRTC replied on July 20. Its report identified several apparent deficits. For example, Radio-Canada was said to have overly centralized its activities in Montreal and Toronto, thereby neglecting the particular needs of the regions. It criticized the fact that the English and French networks worked separately as two distinct services. The CRTC's main criticism overlapped with that of the federalist camp: it found that Radio-Canada had not "contributed to the development of national unity and [had] therefore not fulfilled this important responsibility."[11]

Among the signatories to the report was Jacques Hébert, long-time friend of Pierre Trudeau, with whom he had co-published *Deux innocents en Chine rouge* (*Two Innocents in Red China*).[12]

The report's authors wrote: "Our correspondents, more specifically, accused Radio-Canada of talking too much about Quebec and not enough about the role of francophones outside Quebec. They also criticized the emphasis placed on the 'Quebec nation'[13] in its advertising, its news and commentaries, as well as its exaggerated coverage of the activities of the Parti Québécois."

In spite of everything, the report ended with these words: "Nevertheless, the Commission sincerely believes that CBC/Radio-Canada must stop at nothing to preserve its independence as a source of public information." Not a very convincing conclusion.

Despite the fact that he had been Trudeau's personal choice for the job, CBC/Radio-Canada President Albert Johnson defended Radio-Canada's journalists, and thereby the public broadcaster's independence, in a speech entitled "Freedom and the responsibility of the media":

> The media will always be on trial and we will continuously be called upon to justify our activities. We can never expect to have a tension-free relationship between the media and the different elements of society. For the media, in doing their job of reflecting reality, will always cause sparks, touch nerves, reflect and reveal what we as individuals sometimes would prefer not to know or to see.[14]

The tensions between Canadian nationalists on the one hand and Quebec nationalists on the other were becoming crusades. The tone was becoming more confrontational. At the heart of this struggle, Radio-Canada's journalists tried to reflect events on the ground, among the population, but it was very clear that the pressure on the public broadcaster's journalists was increasing. Here, for example, is an excerpt from an April 1977 interview of André Ouellet, then minister of urban affairs in the Trudeau government, by CBC Radio's Peter Gzowski.

> "I don't want to see Radio-Canada on the fence, presenting, as a neutral body, two sides," Ouellet told Peter Gzowski at the end of April 1977. "Those working there at the time of the referendum should be clearly on the side of the pro-Canada."
>
> "Mr. Ouellet, what if I were using the word propaganda," Gzowski asked.
>
> "Well, when it comes to the survival of our country, I don't think we should be afraid of words."
>
> "Propaganda?" repeated Gzowski, clearly not believing his ears.
>
> "Indeed, sure," Ouellet replied.[15]

The tone had been set. Ideological war justified any means. For André Ouellet, it truly was a war, and as history has taught us, propaganda under such circumstances is widespread. With the arrival of the Parti Québécois in power in 1976, any and all measures would be allowed and members of the federal government would behave like the sole proprietors of Radio-Canada. After all, they had a country to save.

This climate marked the public broadcaster for a long time. Not that the journalists gave way to the demands of the war being waged by the Canadian government against the sovereigntists. But performing what they saw as their duty to rigorously reflect all the various currents of opinion, including those the federalists considered to belong to the "enemy camp," appeared suspicious in the eyes of the so-called owners of the Crown corporation. Simply reflecting the true diversity of opinions in the population was seen as being overly favourable to the sovereigntist side, a betrayal of the mandate to "contribute to the development of national unity." On the other hand, the fact that Radio-Canada's journalists were subject in principle to this mandate to promote Canadian national unity as defined under the law was perceived by many members of the PQ as proof of a federalist bias and of hostility towards their side. Similar problems would arise in the referendums of 1980, 1992, and 1995.

As a result, even impartiality was considered suspicious, leading Marc Thibault to say,

> Need I add that if the duty of impartiality inhibited me personally and unreasonably at Radio-Canada, I preferred my simple right to freedom? Because I prefer information that is free to information that is impartial, should it be the case someday that one opposes the other.[16]

The Parachuting of Pierre C. O'Neil

Impartiality had been given a rough ride, with the surprise appointment of Pierre C. O'Neil as head of television News and Current Affairs in May 1977.

The position included oversight of newscasts and public affairs programming on television. Marc Thibault, who was head of News and Current Affairs programming for all the French-language services, remained O'Neil's superior.

The appointment had created a virtual uprising among the journalists, because O'Neil had been Pierre Trudeau's press secretary from 1972 to 1974. It is true, however, that in his previous journalistic career he had enjoyed a good reputation in the profession.

The man was rather solitary, cultured and congenial in his relationships with others, but also persnickety. If he did not like someone, he could be scathing. However that may be, in 1972, he had chosen to leave journalism and to cozy up to politicians in power. He had begun by offering his services to the federal minister of communications, Gérard

Pelletier, who had hired him to join his team. Several sources attest that the relationship had not gelled and that the minister had suggested that Trudeau hire O'Neil as his press secretary to replace Roméo Leblanc, newly elected as a Liberal MP in October of 1972. O'Neil had therefore been Trudeau's press secretary from 1972 to 1974, during the period when the Liberals had formed a minority government.

It is not surprising that his appointment to the Radio-Canada position in 1977 was perceived as the arrival of the fox in the henhouse. The journalists saw it as a threat to the independence of the News and Current Affairs Service. The Great Wall, the arm's length from political power that was so important to Radio-Canada, was being sacrificed. O'Neil's rapid ascension to the job felt like a strategy manipulated by Ottawa. The objective was, according to some, to stalk the journalists who were accused of harbouring a bias in the debate of the hour: Quebec versus Canada. The solution was to take control of Radio-Canada. But was it really a political order?

It is important to say that O'Neil's appointment was indeed the work of Marc Thibault, the big boss of the News and Information Service. O'Neil had been off in Dakar, Senegal, running a journalism school (CESTI[17]) for the previous two years. Since his departure from the Trudeau entourage, O'Neil had been trying to distance himself and to come back to journalism. Would he ever be able to cleanse himself of his partisan association with Pierre Trudeau?

In his book *Manifeste pour le droit à l'information, de la manipulation à la législation*, journalist Claude Jean Devirieux expresses his belief that the O'Neil appointment had been imposed by the Trudeau government.

> In Canada in 1978, to respond to the accusations that Radio-Canada's News and Information Service had been infiltrated by the indépendantiste element (accusations which had been investigated and proven false), the authorities in Ottawa orchestrated the nomination of the former press secretary to the Prime Minister of Canada, Pierre Elliott Trudeau, Pierre O'Neil, a career journalist, in the hope that the newscasts and current

affairs programming would conform more strictly to the national unity policy. It is interesting to note that at the time, only the Toronto papers had flagged the questionable nature of such an appointment.[18]

André Payette, one of Radio-Canada's star hosts at the time, shares Devirieux's interpretation of events: "I always thought that the appointment had been imposed by the Liberals. I don't believe that it was Marc Thibault's initiative, it would be most unlike him."[19] André Payette is insistent on this point: the O'Neil appointment had been imposed by the political powers that be.

One of Thibault's close associates, Mario Cardinal,[20] agrees that it very unlikely that Pierre O'Neil had truly been his boss's choice:

> Thibault fought so hard for Radio-Canada's News and Current Affairs to remain neutral in the face of all kinds of political machinations that I find it hard to believe that all of a sudden, he would have chosen Pierre O'Neil to become the head of News and Current Affairs. I've always harboured a serious doubt about this.[21]

On the other hand, another interpretation is that Thibault had sought to calm down Trudeau's Quebec caucus by offering the job of head of television News and Current Affairs to a known federalist. "Thibault appointed Pierre O'Neil to protect himself," says Réal Barnabé, another close associate of Thibault's in 1977. According to him, Thibault felt that the appointment would blunt the many attacks to which the political powers in Ottawa had subjected him. O'Neil's presence at his side would establish that Radio-Canada was not a "nest of separatists," as many federal Liberal MPs kept calling it. However, Réal Barnabé adds, "We must remember that Gérard Pelletier was minister of communications at the time of the O'Neil appointment. I see Pelletier as a defender of Radio-Canada's independence, not the opposite."[22] Paul Larose, another member of the management team close to Thibault, agrees:

For the Marc Thibault that I knew, it seems to me absolutely impossible that he would accept the imposition of
that appointment by Ottawa. The links between Pierre
O'Neil and Pierre E. Trudeau's office were too widely
known to [allow us] to think that Marc Thibault would
not have taken the time to weigh the pros and cons of
this appointment.[23]

Marc Thibault's daughter, Sophie, now the main news anchor at
TVA, is of the same opinion. She does not see how her father could
have allowed the imposition of such an appointment. "It was really not
his style! He would never have accepted it."[24] She adds that her father
actually had a lot of respect for Pierre O'Neil, as a journalist and as an
individual. She also says that she believes Thibault was well aware of the
way the appointment would be perceived, but that he maintained that
Pierre O'Neil had many great qualities.

Jean Giroux knew Pierre O'Neil well, as they had worked together
at CESTI from 1975 to 1977, then at Radio-Canada from 1978 to 1985.
He believes that Thibault hired O'Neil to counter the Liberal machine
and its never-ending attacks against Radio-Canada's News and Current
Affairs service:

For me, there is only one thesis. He had no choice; it was
the only way to put a brake on the Liberal machine that
wanted to control Radio-Canada.... I have difficulty
believing that O'Neil could have been imposed. Marc
Thibault was not the kind of person to allow others to
tell him what to do. He simply understood that he had
no choice.... Thibault decided that he would not undertake a losing battle and that he would use O'Neil as a
lightning rod. And in addition to that, we all had great
respect for O'Neil as a journalist.[25]

One thing is certain: Thibault did indeed need a lightning rod to
deal with the many attacks coming his way. In 1978, he was summoned

to appear before the CRTC to "reaffirm the principles of journalistic neutrality on the eve of the 1980 referendum."[26]

If the Liberals elected to Quebec City and to Ottawa saw Radio-Canada as a "nest of separatists," many journalists at Radio-Canada subscribed more to the theory of a federalist plot. Later, in the 1990s, the believers in this theory saw in the appointment of Pierre O'Neil as the confirmation of their suspicions, and they saw further confirmation in his subsequent appointment, after leaving Radio-Canada, as head of the Centre for Research and Information on Canada. This was a creation of the Council for Canadian Unity, an organization devoted to, among other things, the promotion of federal institutions. We heard a lot about the organization during the 1995 referendum period, and again during the Gomery Commission inquiry into the sponsorship scandal.[27]

So, was this a strategic choice by Marc Thibault or a command performance? We'll probably never get to the bottom of this story, its principal protagonists having taken their secrets with them to the grave.

The End of Ads on Radio

The 1970s also saw another landmark decision in the history of CBC/Radio-Canada. In 1974, the CRTC ordered the public broadcaster to end advertising on its radio services. Since then, the absence of advertising has been part of CBC/Radio-Canada's DNA and has helped to differentiate it from the private stations. Some people talk about a "CBC sound" or a "Radio-Canada sound," which gives listeners shelter from noisy ads. This sound is now available only on Radio 1 and La Première Chaîne, since the CRTC's 2013 approval, at the request of the president, Hubert Lacroix, of a return to advertising on ICI Musique and Radio Two.

Unfortunately, the CRTC's 1974 radio decision was never extended to television. Too bad! It would have been worthwhile to promote the philosophy that underlies all public service.

CBC/Radio-Canada management should have insisted that this debate take place. On the French side, they were much more preoccupied with the increasing popularity of Télé-Métropole. Believing it would be sufficient to continue playing the competition and performance game, they lost the opportunity to reflect on what should truly distinguish public television from private television. They had great difficulty accepting the loss of viewers to an increasingly powerful competitor.

Nevertheless, the following decade would confirm that rival's power, as it took pleasure in crowing about its audience numbers. In 1973, la Maison de Radio-Canada had opened just a short distance away from Télé-Métropole. Since then, there had always been references to *le concurrent d'en face* ("the competition from across the street").

CHAPTER 5

Pierre Trudeau Promises Change

On the night of May 20, 1980, Bernard Derome announced, "At 7:55 p.m., the trend in the results gathered in the last few minutes by Radio-Canada leads us to conclude that the 'no' option will win the referendum." When the final results were in, the "no" had attracted 59.56 percent and the "yes" 40.44 percent of the vote.

In his last speech of the referendum campaign, on May 14, at Paul Sauvé Arena in Montreal, the prime minister of Canada, Pierre Trudeau, had told the people of Quebec,

> Here, and I make a solemn declaration to all Canadians in the other provinces, we, the Quebec MPs, are laying ourselves on the line, because we are telling Quebecers to vote NO and telling you in the other provinces that we will not agree to your interpreting a NO vote as an indication that everything is fine and can remain as it was before. We want change and we are willing to lay our seats in the House on the line to have change.

The Post-Referendum Settling of Scores

One thing is certain: after the May 1980 referendum, senior management jobs in the French network were also on the line. We can see this clearly in the personal notes of Raymond David, the vice-president of French

Services at the time, which members of his family have made available to me, for which I thank them.

The following excerpts from his diary are interesting:

> August 8th, 1980 — Meeting with the President [Al Johnson]. Surprised to see that Marc [Thibault] will not be leaving on sabbatical in September, to be replaced by Pierre O'Neil.…

> January 15th, 1981 — The Pres. authorises me to name O'Neil as Marc's associate and to open a dialogue with Michel Roy with a view to replacing O'Neil.…

> August 3rd, 1981 — Back from vacation. The President is urging Jacques L. [Landry, Raymond David's EA] to appoint O'Neil right away, before September "because they are saying that there will be changes". I am supposed to call Johnson soon to let them know what I have done about this.[1]

So the president of CBC/Radio-Canada, Albert Wesley Johnson, was insisting that Thibault give over his position to Pierre O'Neil, "because they are saying that there will be changes." The only logical interpretation of these words is that Johnson had promised the government that there would be a change in the senior management of News and Current Affairs in the French network. According to the information I have been able to uncover, it seems that by doing this, Johnson was trying to obtain a renewal of his own mandate as president of the corporation. It seems that he thought his chances were good. After all, he was well acquainted with Pierre Trudeau, who had appointed him in the first place. He was also a personal friend of Michael Pitfield, clerk of the Privy Council and Trudeau's cabinet secretary from 1980 to 1982. Promoting O'Neil as overall head of the French network's News and Current Affairs was part of his plan.

During this period, the "holy war" between federalists and sovereigntists had reached a fever pitch. Raymond David's notes also reveal that the promised changes included his own departure from his position as vice-president. Neither he nor his friend and colleague Marc Thibault, were well liked at the top. In his notes, David relays a chilling comment from the president, on February 27, 1980: "Johnson said: 'You know very well that they don't trust you, Marc and you?'"

Raymond David was one of the great leaders in the history of Radio-Canada. He had defended the independence[2] of the public broadcaster, but he had also been in favour of the autonomy of the French-language services within the corporation. In 1980, the president of CBC/Radio-Canada and members of the board were pressuring him to resign and to leave his position, which he steadfastly refused to do, according to his diary. On August 8, 1980, almost three months after the referendum, he noted that President Johnson had even picked his successor: Pierre Desroches. Upon learning the news, David answered the president: "It is not justified and unjust after everything I have done for the Corporation over the last 30 years." He quotes Johnson's retort: "I appreciate you and I admire you, it's hard for both of us." David says he understood that Johnson wanted to make a change before his own departure. "For one reason only: he is leaving [his job] in two years. Putting a new management in place. A new Vice President establishes a new outlook."

For Johnson, making these changes was the key to his strategy for being renewed as president of the Crown corporation.

Further on in his diary, on October 14, 1980, David was firm about his intentions. He would not resign: "Long conversation with the Pres. Told him I would leave [my position] the day after my replacement, and that I would not resign. It's a question of dignity, of honour. That I had consulted my wife, that I would find myself another job. 'It's your decision, but it's my life.'"

There was tension between the two men, as we can see in this further note:

> Nov. 13th, 1980 – Telephone conversations. Pres., Marc [Thibault], Pierre [Desroches] and me: in preparation for the Vastel article, I asked the President, if I am asked,

'Are you being asked to leave Radio-Canada? What do I answer? No?' He said: 'That's what I'll say too.' The silences were heavy.

The article by Michel Vastel was published on November 15, 1980. It reported the rumour of an attempted housecleaning at the top of Radio-Canada's French networks. The telephone conversations were therefore about trying to soften the impact of any possible revelations by Vastel.

On January 6, 1981, David described the political context of the period, in which wild rumours flourished:

> Marc [Thibault] tells me that O'Neil heard the follow-ing rumour from Michel Roy[3]: someone high up in the Liberal Party told him that the President intended to get rid of me between February and April of this year.

Nevertheless, neither departures nor appointments would be announced for another year. It was not until January 29, 1982, that David would write,

> I have alerted my colleagues that I am leaving [my posi-tion] on April 1st. I will retire on July 1st, after reaching an agreement with the President. I have emphasized that he must not delay in naming Pierre [Desroches] – at most two weeks. He is of the view that in my shoes, he would simply retire.

But his departure was delayed yet again. On February 23, 1982, David came up with his own explanation of the situation:

> Still no appointment. Pitfield says he has spoken to Fox[4] and Durand proposes to wait until the end of March to appoint someone. It smells of politics and it illuminates things clearly.

This last note from the former vice-president of Radio-Canada is a good illustration of the tensions that senior management of the French network faced at the time. The idea of Radio-Canada's arm's length from political power seemed damaged in these tumultuous years.

In 1982, the contract of the president of CBC/Radio-Canada, Al Johnson, was not renewed. He had believed for a while that the changes he was making would demonstrate that he had the situation well in hand and that he was the candidate for change ... but his efforts were in vain. The real candidate for change in the eyes of the Trudeau government had already been chosen. It was to be Pierre Juneau, a close friend of Trudeau's who was already deputy minister of communications under Francis Fox. Pierre Juneau became the new president and CEO of CBC/Radio-Canada. "He wanted the job. He obtained it over lunch with Pierre Trudeau," Francis Fox told me during a meeting I requested during the preparation of this book.[5]

For their part, the two friends and colleagues, Raymond David and Marc Thibault, also left Radio-Canada in 1982. Pierre O'Neil did become overall head of News and Current Affairs on the French side, a position he retained until 1991. These were the changes that mattered at the time. As for the former minister of communications, Francis Fox, he denies that he meddled in Radio-Canada's affairs during the Johnson presidency. "He [Johnson] wasn't the kind of guy to allow himself to be influenced. He was Trudeau's man."[6]

Raymond David's notes have the merit of showing that there absolutely was political pressure, but from where? The government of the day was far from content to name the president and CEO of CBC/Radio-Canada and the members of its board, as provided by law. The political interventions in the choice of the corporation's mandate went far beyond that. History would repeat itself three decades later.

An Attempted Putsch by Journalists in Ottawa?

The fallout from the referendum would last for many years, and the war of the nationalisms was far from over. Neither was the difficulty of practising journalism at Radio-Canada.

After the defeat of the "yes" option, René Lévesque renewed his hold on power in the Quebec election of April 13, 1981; it was as if the people of Quebec wanted an insurance policy in the major round of constitutional negotiations that was starting up.

The Parti Québécois won eighty seats, versus forty-two for Claude Ryan's Liberals. On election night, someone was missing: Bernard Derome. For once, he was not at his anchor desk. There are no archives of that election coverage on television, because the news staff at Radio-Canada had been on strike since October 30, 1980. This strike, which lasted until June 29, 1981, affected the newsroom for a long time. The strike began because the journalists, whose union was part of the CSN (sometimes called the Confederation of National Trade Unions, or CNTU, in English) wanted to obtain the same improved working conditions that already existed in other major Quebec media outlets and in the provincial civil service. Certain gains obtained through this strike, such as maternity leave and slightly better vacation provisions, were subsequently extended to the entire federal civil service.

The union members also wanted jurisdictional changes. They wanted to limit management's ability to impose editorial decisions. They wanted to exercise the same control over newscasts as producers had over programs. This is the issue that got the most media coverage and that led to the portrayal of the conflict as a struggle for freedom of information.

In reading Raymond David's notes, it becomes obvious how fragile the position of the French network's management had become, and it is also clear that at the time, the vast majority of the journalists were completely unaware of this.

On top of everything else, while his Montreal colleagues were on strike, Paul Racine, Radio-Canada's parliamentary bureau chief in Ottawa and a member of a different union, was energetically beavering away. Indeed, Racine was suspected of having led an attempted putsch[7] against Radio-Canada's senior management, including the head of News and Current Affairs, Marc Thibault.

But Paul Racine denies this:

Don't be ridiculous! Don't be ridiculous! The truth is that year, I was really at loggerheads with Radio-Canada's management and I said so publicly. It was a long quarrel and I never denied that. So, I was reproached about it. The rumours about a putsch are a symptom of management's paranoia at the time. But there was never any substance to such a putsch. There were only open and public criticisms.[8]

Paul Racine and a few colleagues from Radio-Canada's Ottawa bureau did not hesitate to criticize, openly, what they thought was a lack of leadership in their senior management, which was in no hurry to upgrade the French network's equipment and modernize Radio-Canada's political coverage. Racine continued:

One day, I got a call from Pierre O'Neil, who was panicking because the French network, unlike the English network, was not adequately organized. Live broadcast coverage of the House of Commons was about to begin and we weren't even ready![9]

Several journalists had a difficult relationship with members of senior management in the News and Current Affairs Service, and occasionally defied them. The conflict with the unionized journalists from the CSN was symptomatic of this state of affairs. But what about the supposed attempted putsch? For some, it represented an intergenerational conflict; others saw it as justified criticism, given that the French network was so far behind; yet others had personal ambitions or could have been conspiring with Liberal politicians. There was certainly unhappiness with Thibault's management style. And some of the ambitious players were unscrupulous.

"We were young and ambitious," said Racine. "We compared ourselves with our CBC colleagues and we could see that we had fallen behind."[10] As Radio-Canada's parliamentary correspondent, Racine had contacts in Ottawa, and not just any contacts. Like any good reporter on Parliament Hill, he had developed relationships with a number of Liberals, including Robert Gourd, MP for Argenteuil, who chaired the House of Commons Standing Committee for Communications and Culture, and the minister of communications, Francis Fox. Racine was accused of having conspired with the Liberal MPs who had led the charge against Marc Thibault.

In November 1980, during the journalists' strike, Liberal MPs Robert Gourd, Jacques Olivier, and Serge Joyal, all members of the Parliamentary Committee on Communications and Culture, had even summoned Marc Thibault to appear before them and had criticized him severely. They had obtained several internal memos from his department, which they quoted abundantly. Rumour had it that those behind the attempted putsch had leaked the memos to the committee.

Paul Racine denies this:

> Robert Gourd and the other MPs only repeated what I and my journalist colleagues had discussed at our table at the Press Club in Ottawa. They could hear us talking. We talked to all the politicians. As for Francis Fox, I used to meet him at the Press Club too. He wasn't a friend, but an acquaintance. And knowing him, I can tell you that Fox was not a minister to orchestrate a putsch.[11]

At the same time, Francis Fox declared that it was high time to do an in-depth analysis of the News and Current Affairs sector of Radio-Canada. The coincidence of all these actions certainly conveyed the impression that there was a conspiracy. Several journalists wrote articles on the subject in November 1980.

Despite the political pressures, Thibault did not change his position. For him, it was out of the question to give in to political interference in the management of his News and Current Affairs Service. The striking journalists certainly had much about which to reproach their ultimate boss, particularly when it came to his attitude with regard to labour relations. However, few of them would have supported the idea of taking up with politicians to get rid of him. This in no way dissuaded Paul Racine.

As for Francis Fox, he denies having participated in such an attempt.[12] Of course, he listened to the complaints of Radio-Canada journalists like Racine with great interest. Some may have interpreted this very interested and sympathetic hearing as outright support. It is certainly the case that this open public criticism gave the federal MPs plenty of ammunition, which they did not hesitate to use against the senior management of News and Current Affairs.

It is also true that Thibault was a fierce defender of the independence of both Radio-Canada as a whole and its News and Current Affairs Service. This was not surprising. The man had principles, and he was nobody's lapdog. His daughter Sophie remembers conversations at home in which he spoke with conviction of his resistance to attacks and of the principle of independence of the News and Current Affairs service. "In spite of all the attacks and pressures," she says, "my father always defended his journalists with conviction."[13]

On November 15, 1980, Marc Laurendeau, then a contributing columnist at *La Presse*, wrote about this supposed attempted putsch:

> Marc Thibault often stood up to the CRTC, and with admirable inflexibility when it came to protecting freedom of information for journalists against the wild interventions from certain CRTC commissioners. Those who are plotting to get him into hot water or to push him out could find themselves (and this is the most likely outcome, according to the names being bandied about) with a head of News and Current Affairs who would be much more compliant and accommodating to the vengeful reactions of the federal MPs.[14]

Louise Cousineau, the television critic *at La Presse*, confronted Paul Racine directly at the time. Her column was headlined: "Paul Racine denies being a 'putschiste'". The latter affirmed that he had never predicted but simply "wished" that "the heads of the bosses at the News and Current Affairs service would roll between now and Christmas."[15]

Today, Racine remembers this interview very well, because it was a landmark moment in his career. "It is true that we wanted things to change," he explains. "For years, a group of young journalists — myself, François Perrault, Normand Lester[16] — we wanted to modernize Radio-Canada."[17]

According to a number of witnesses in whom he confided at the time, Racine was convinced that he could run Radio-Canada's News and Current Affairs Service and do a far better job than Thibault and his team.

At the time, journalist Réal Barnabé was interviewed on the current affairs show *Ce soir*, which was still on the air despite the news journalists' strike because its staff belonged to a different union. Barnabé's work often took him to Ottawa, where he would run into Racine. He recalled:

> A few days before the [Marc] Thibault intervention, Paul [Racine] told me that his appointment to Montreal was imminent. I even seem to remember that he saw himself as Vice President of French Services with François [Perrault] as head of News and Current Affairs.[18]

That was the last straw. With his position already fragile because of the journalists' strike in Montreal, Thibault had to react quickly. When he found out what was going on, he summoned Racine to a disciplinary meeting in Montreal. Thibault felt that it was his duty to protect the independence of his service from political power. Paul Racine did not try to defend himself. He confirmed having made the remarks quoted by Louise Cousineau in *La Presse*. In fact, he strongly believed that the senior management of News and Current Affairs was not up to the new challenges, especially those that were coming with new methods of television production. Racine resigned in December 1980. At the meeting, he says, were O'Neil, Thibault, and someone from human resources. "I negotiated my departure, and resigning did not cause me to lose my accumulated [retirement] benefits as an employee of Radio-Canada."[19]

He left Radio-Canada, and eighteen months later he accepted an invitation from Francis Fox to join him at the Department of

Communications, which was responsible for, among other things, Radio-Canada. "I'm the one who recruited him after his departure from Radio-Canada. I never regretted it. He did a good job at the Department, even after our defeat at the hands of the Progressive Conservatives in 1984,"[20] Fox emphasized.

In his personal notes, David describes the discussions around the resignation of Racine. He even seems to have used this "putsch affair" in his own negotiations with the president:

> November 25th, 1980 — Lunch at the Ritz with the Pres. He asks me again to leave my position. Talks to me about the job of VP of International Relations. I tell him that given all the public talk about a putsch, no one will believe this, and that he will come off as having submitted to the will of the politicians. I ask him: "Why are you so stubborn?" It's a difficult lunch. He has Michel Roy's editorial in front of him. He tells me: "He backed me into a corner." He says that I am paralysing him, that he can't manoeuver and find a replacement for me. Same old conversation as the previous times.

The Michel Roy editorial the president referred to was published in the November 26, 1980, edition of *Le Devoir*.[21] Roy vigorously denounced the attempted putsch against senior management of French Services at Radio-Canada:

> The reformers had in effect organized to collude with the politicians, convinced that a timely intervention from the men in power would be enough to trigger the desired changes.... Let's not dwell on the distasteful character of the process that led journalists to this kind of despicable scheming. It's the stuff of comic opera that we could smile about if it didn't lead to the grave danger of bringing in the reign of the arbitrary in an area where power — and we have seen it in other countries — has

trouble resisting the temptation to subjugate the news by entrusting it to devoted henchmen.[22]

A bit further, Roy adds a few words about Johnson that may explain why he felt cornered: "Mr. Al Johnson, who is usually talkative when it comes time to defend his senior management, has been entirely mute in this affair which has unfolded virtually under his nose."[23]

If Raymond David's personal notes are to be believed, the rumours of a putsch were useful in delaying his own departure, so desired by the president of CBC/Radio-Canada: "December 2nd, 1980 — Endless back-and-forth about Racine. Michèle Lasnier[24] tells me that on October 25th, Jeanne Sauvé[25] had consulted her about the type of person who should replace me."

Further on in his notes, David writes about the conclusion of the putsch affair associated with Racine: "December 19th, 1980 — Racine's resignation. Obtained through secret wheeling and dealing with the President. He says that Fox was not involved in the coup, i.e. that he had not spoken to them."

We will never know to which secret wheeling and dealing David was referring. The principal person involved, Paul Racine, has only this to say:

> The journalists in Montreal had been on strike for several months already, our income had been cut in half because of the lack of work in Ottawa; the climate was really unhealthy. I decided to leave [Radio-Canada] and to work elsewhere.... Senior management believed in the putsch theory. Al Johnson was a friend of Pitfield. Marc Thibault and Raymond David also believed in the putsch theory.[26]

In hindsight, one thing is blindingly obvious: the independence of a public broadcaster is always fragile. In order to preserve it, it is essential for not only senior management but also journalists to understand that they must constantly maintain a healthy distance from the political powers that be.

The Confirmation of Pierre O'Neil

As for Marc Thibault, he remained on the job until September 1, 1981. Partly because he was just tired of the whole thing, but mostly — according to members of his inner circle who confided in me — because he wanted to spend more time with his wife, stricken with multiple sclerosis, he retired entirely in 1982, along with his faithful friend and boss, Raymond David. It was the end of an era at Radio-Canada.

Was Thibault simply obsolete? There was certainly an intergenerational conflict, Racine explains, but also conflicting visions about television between the old-school senior management and the restless younger people.

Be that as it may, Thibault left big shoes to fill at Radio-Canada: a great journalistic culture, strong ethics, and, most importantly, constant vigilance on the issue of independence and the necessary arm's length between the public broadcaster and the government of the day. The next generation of journalists has held up these principles like a shield against those who attack Radio-Canada's News and Current Affairs. This is really Thibault's legacy.[27] On September 14, 1981, Radio-Canada announced the appointment of Thibault's successor, Pierre O'Neil, as director-general of News and Current Affairs for both radio and television. It was the dawn of a new era.

Throughout his time at the top, the label of "former press secretary to Pierre Trudeau" was indelibly attached to O'Neil. He was always on the defensive with his management colleagues on the subject of the hidden political agenda said to have been behind his appointment. Many of them remember that he always affirmed that he did not have a political mandate. And, he would add, a person can certainly be a journalist, a federalist, and defend Radio-Canada's impartiality and independence. It is fair to ask whether he would have found it acceptable if a sovereigntist journalist had been appointed to his job. Let's be clear here: it is obvious that journalists and those who manage them are not disembodied spirits.

Journalistic neutrality has never meant that journalists are not entitled to hold personal political opinions. I have always thought that it matters little whether a news director in the public service was federalist or sovereigntist, of the left or the right. What matters is that the person is a journalist and that he or she is not showing his or her true colours on the job. In my opinion, the most important quality in a journalist is doubt, the ability to question everything one hears. And, I would add, that includes questioning one's own convictions. A public broadcaster must be obsessed with showcasing a diversity of opinions.

What we are talking about here is really proximity to political power. In speaking regularly with former political colleagues whose mission is to influence, someone who manages a News and Current Affairs Service becomes vulnerable to that influence. We will return to that subject.

How did Radio-Canada's journalists react to the arrival of their new boss? Madeleine Poulin knew Pierre O'Neil well. He had been her superior in her time as a parliamentary correspondent in Ottawa, a Paris correspondent, and host of Radio-Canada shows such as *Le Point* and *Le Point médias*. Poulin says,

> Many of the journalists saw the appointment as the installation of some kind of overseer with a direct mandate from Pierre Trudeau. At first, I thought this reaction was a little paranoid, but over time I had to admit that Pierre O'Neil really did behave like some kind of guardian of an orthodoxy. In fact, he behaved as if this orthodoxy was threatened by the very journalists he had to manage. Throughout his entire time in the job, the news service was under his strict, proactive and mostly, perpetually worried surveillance. Pierre O'Neil was wary of all journalists. In this chilly climate, in addition to their duty of impartiality, the journalists found that they were straitjacketed by a duty of extreme reserve in all circumstances. After his departure, the environment became gradually more relaxed.[28]

I worked with Madeleine Poulin as producer of *Le Point* from 1986 to 1992. I can confirm her observations. We felt that we were constantly under surveillance. Even in the daily production meetings, where we discussed the choice of subjects and guests, we felt that the slightest editorial remark could be distorted by our bosses. We always had our guard up.

I don't mean to say here that it would be a good thing for journalists to express their political opinions freely at work. On the contrary, I believe that the habit of reserve makes the exercise of impartiality easier, opens up easier access to sources, and underpins greater journalistic freedom. Nevertheless, an excess of prudence can paralyze.

CHAPTER 6

1984 — Marcel Masse and Pierre Juneau

Before the Progressive Conservatives came to power in September 1984, Francis Fox, the minister of communications, had tabled a new orientation document for CBC/Radio-Canada, *Building the Future: Towards a Distinctive CBC*.[1] It has not been sufficiently acknowledged that the document advocated an unequivocal commitment to CBC/Radio-Canada, Fox emphasizes.[2]

While insisting that CBC/Radio-Canada should provide a "much more distinctive service — a clear-cut Canadian broadcasting alternative to private broadcasters," the document also emphasized commercialization. Some people saw this as a contradiction.

"As a means of supplementing its Parliamentary appropriation, the government believes the CBC should be aggressively involved in the sale for a profit of its programming and related cultural products ..."[3] The document was once again forceful on the subject of Radio-Canada's role in promoting national unity:

> The phrase in the CBC mandate, "contribute to the development of national unity," is deemed to mean being "consciously partial to the success of Canada as a united country with its own national objectives, independent from those of other countries," while maintaining the highest standards of professional journalism.[4]

Radio-Canada's journalists clearly understood this major contradiction. The wording of the document constrained them to the idea of building a strong, united Canada. This made it very difficult to practise impartial journalism in a society as divided as the Quebec of that time. Even today, Fox denies that he wanted to support a propaganda operation: "We wanted to promote Canadian values. It was not our intent to push propaganda." He maintains that within these values, it was important to have high-quality journalism, meeting the highest professional standards and offering complete independence to the people working in News and Current Affairs: "The document was misunderstood. I can understand the discomfort of the journalists. Even the former president, Al Johnson, told me after leaving his position that he was in complete disagreement with the wording of the mandate." Fox also emphasizes that the new policy had the merit of clearly defining the issues of the time: "We had to put the cable distributors at the heart of the new broadcasting system. We did that. We had to support the development of independent producers in a way that would complement what CBC/Radio-Canada was producing. We did that too, which led to the creation of a flourishing film and television industry in Montreal."[5]

The Arrival of Pierre Juneau

There have been many influential people at Radio-Canada with close ties to the Liberal Party. And this has led to many complaints. So it was with the appointment in 1982 of Pierre Juneau as president and CEO of CBC/Radio-Canada, which triggered accusations of partisanship among sovereigntists as well as Conservatives.

Pierre Juneau was indeed a well-known federalist and had been defeated in 1975 as the Liberal candidate in the riding of Hochelaga-Maisonneuve. He was even, briefly, the unelected minister of communications, following the appointment of his friend Gérard Pelletier as Canada's ambassador to Paris. Juneau had also been one of the original founders of *Cité Libre* magazine, along with Gérard Pelletier and Pierre Trudeau.

That being said, he did not have the profile of a typical partisan. For one thing, he had worked for seventeen years at the National Film Board. He was a great defender of francophone culture. He had also made his mark as chair of the CRTC from 1968 to 1975. We owe to him the existence of certain regulatory measures to protect Canadian ownership of the media. The imposition of Canadian content quotas on all Canadian radio and television outlets was also his doing. So when he was appointed president of CBC/Radio-Canada, no one could question his competence. "Pierre Juneau was the incarnation of the defender of public broadcasting,"[6] says Florian Sauvageau, professor emeritus of journalism at Laval University and director of the Centre d'études sur les médias (Centre for Media Studies).

When Brian Mulroney's Progressive Conservative Party took power in September 1984, many thought that Juneau's days at the top of CBC/Radio-Canada were numbered. Juneau himself had fostered the rumour that he would refuse to resign before the end of his mandate if he were asked, both on principle and to protect the independence of the institution vis-à-vis the government of the day. This was entirely legitimate.

In 1984, Marcel Masse became minister of communications in the first Mulroney cabinet. He denied having pressured Juneau to resign. Here are a few excerpts from an interview he granted me on June 3, 2014:

> Masse: After the election in the fall of 1984, I started by becoming familiar with the files in my department. Then, as minister, I met several times with Mr. Juneau, at least once a month.

> Saulnier: Your relationship was good?

> Masse: Excellent, I insist, excellent. Independently of what the newspapers were saying. You know, the cultural community always feels under siege. Radio-Canada always feels that it's being attacked. And with regard to my relationship with Juneau: he was a gentleman, Juneau! No problem between us. But how do you stop rumours?

You're not going to call a press conference and put your arm around him. But that said, there are always budget cuts here and there. But when he and I had discussions, they were always about Radio-Canada and its mandate.

Marcel Masse's Great Battle

According to Marcel Masse, Radio-Canada's real challenge in 1984 was the definition of the mandate and the mission of the public broadcaster. The former minister recognizes that there was a divergence of views on the subject between Pierre Juneau and himself, but never to the point of asking him to tender his resignation. The president of the corporation insisted on defining the mandate according to the old advertising slogan: "Radio-Canada. Everything for everyone." Masse disagreed with this. He thought it was just a smokescreen to hide CBC/Radio-Canada management's perpetual obsession with ratings and popularity, imitating the private broadcasters. "I was accused of being an elitist," says Masse. "It's not just that! Our role is to elevate the public discourse. You won't succeed in higher achievements by imitating others."[7]

The Conservative minister always asked the question:

> Why weren't there more teleplays, more concerts on Radio-Canada? Obviously, I could not intervene in programming matters, out of respect for the independence of the public broadcaster. But at the same time, I would have so wanted for Radio-Canada to distinguish itself through its cultural programming.

These are the themes on which he disagreed with CBC/Radio-Canada management, says Masse:

> I [told Pierre Juneau] that there was too much News and Current Affairs and not enough culture on Radio-Canada. Is it a vehicle for production and

dissemination of culture, or for News and Current
Affairs? And I would tell him, the more time passes,
the fewer programs there are on literature. For me,
Radio-Canada is four things: culture and information,
the two biggest pieces. Then, lower down in the hier-
archy, two other big pieces: a public institution and its
relationship with advertising. We have to find the right
balance in all this.

In his opinion, Radio-Canada had lost sight of its priority, which
should be to produce and broadcast high-quality cultural programming.
Instead, according to him, there was a tendency to inflate advertising
revenues with shows that did not really set themselves apart from those
of the competition.

The former minister also thought that as events unfolded, he was
proven to have been right. He explains:

Radio-Canada has allowed its cultural mandate to
atrophy virtually down to zero. That was my debate
with Pierre Juneau. You want to respect the independence of the public broadcaster, but at the same time,
as the minister, you want to change the mandate. It
wasn't simple.

When we talked in 2014, Marcel Masse was still upset that in 1981
no one appeared to have opposed the appointment of a former Trudeau
press secretary, Pierre O'Neil, as head of all of Radio-Canada's News and
Current Affairs. "It's absolutely unbelievable!"

As a member of Mulroney's Progressive Conservative cabinet
from Quebec, Masse also had another avowed objective with regard to
Radio-Canada:

I had come back to politics with Brian Mulroney for the
constitution. In the constitution, Radio-Canada was a
fly in the ointment. Its mandate to make propaganda

— I don't remember the exact wording of the law[8] — but to "promote national unity" it made no sense! That definition was about propaganda! I told myself that if I, who was very pro-Quebec, if I didn't undertake this fight, no one would. It was a question of principle!

It was Masse's first really big fight inside the government as minister of communications. He faced stiff opposition both inside the PC caucus and, of course, from the other parties; in addition, there was the uphill challenge of obtaining ratification from the Liberal-dominated Senate of the time.

Changing such a law was no small thing. To get there, you had to find the right alternative approach. Masse then had an idea. Why not take inspiration from the mandate of the National Film Board, adopted in 1968: "to interpret Canada to Canadians and to other nations"? As he says, "I thought reluctant MPs and Senators would find it more acceptable to draw on the NFB's mandate to define one for CBC/Radio-Canada."

Masse took on this battle after a three-year stint at the Department of Energy (1986–1989); his return to the Department of Communications (1989–1991) aimed to see through the final adoption of the 1991 Broadcasting Act. The new act said, "… the programming provided by the Corporation should (i) be predominantly and distinctively Canadian, (ii) reflect Canada and its regions to national and regional audiences while serving the special needs of those regions …."[9] The promotion of national unity was out.

As Marcel Masse's assistant deputy minister of communications, Richard Stursberg[10] was responsible for the clause-by-clause study of the new Broadcasting Act by the House of Commons Standing Committee on Communications. He confirms that Masse was continually preoccupied with the wording of the law with regard to CBC/Radio-Canada: "We discussed the role of CBC/Radio-Canada many times with Mr. Masse. He always insisted on the wording 'reflect the country' and to drop the words 'promote national unity.'"[11]

Pierre O'Neil's Imprint

In a memo to managers in News and Current Affairs, which predates the adoption of the new act, Pierre O'Neil had this to say:

> On the occasion of the tabling of the proposed new Broadcasting Act, some have pointed out with satisfaction, even relief, the replacement of the portion of the mandate that directed Radio-Canada to "contribute to the development of national unity". In doing so, some are trying to break down open doors…. [It] was always a given that in these matters news and information had the obligation to present a generous diversity of points of view. In other words, it was agreed that adequately reflecting the country as a whole was the best possible contribution to resolving, whatever form that would take, political conflicts.[12]

By using the expression "trying to break down open doors," O'Neil was probably attempting to downplay the impact that the ambiguity — the reference to national unity in the act — had always had on the work of journalists.

If Marcel Masse was trying to break down open doors, what about others? Réal Barnabé remembers well his time as a young manager reporting to O'Neil:

> He reproached us mostly for professional failings. He never dared make direct, or shall we say partisan interventions. Sometimes, he would tell me orally: "André [Ouellet] called me" or "Marc [Lalonde[13]] telephoned me, and there is such and such a problem." I can assure you that I never followed up on these observations with the news desk. Marcel Desjardins, whom I had recruited as my deputy when the Montréal-Matin closed down, replaced me in April or May of 1981. You knew Marcel. A rock. In his own way, he also knew how to manage O'Neil.[14]

This sums up the reaction of the vast majority of journalists and managers in News and Current Affairs while working in this environment: do your job while ignoring the pressure, regardless of its source.

O'Neil also showed his true colours in January 1989 when Premier Robert Bourassa wanted to invoke the "notwithstanding clause" after the Supreme Court had struck down a portion of Quebec's language law, Bill 101,[15] with regard to the language of commercial signs:

> I am not questioning the legality nor the legitimacy of the "notwithstanding clause".... However, I continue to be offended that a whole class of journalists — ours — is so easily accommodated, and considers it a moderate position, to suspend rights pretty much indefinitely..., I'm not saying that it's up to us to do battle. But I remain deeply convinced that we do have the duty to review all our programming to ensure that it makes as much room as possible for the contesting of this suspension of rights.[16]

According to several witnesses, O'Neil often wrote these kinds of memos to the managers in News and Current Affairs. I have only been able to get my hands on a few examples.

Throughout O'Neil's time in office, there was a kind of fog of Liberal influence that was felt in the appointment of certain senior managers with Liberal associations. Some appointments of producers and journalists were also surprising.

For example, Lina Allard, former chief of staff to Claude Ryan from 1981 to 1982, who started at Radio-Canada in January 1983, oversaw the public affairs program *Le Point* in 1988. Then there was Patrick Parisot, who worked from April 1991 on as editor-in-chief after being promoted exceptionally quickly. He left *Le Point* in 1992 and was shortly thereafter appointed Jean Chrétien's press secretary during the referendum campaign. For most of those who had worked with him, this came as no surprise.

Catherine Cano, who had been John Turner's press secretary from 1986 to 1989, was hired at Radio-Canada's Washington bureau shortly after leaving her job in Ottawa, first as an assistant in administration then later on in production. Normally, the rule at Radio-Canada is to require a two-year period of "purgatory" before hiring people who have worked for political parties, but rules can be less strict in foreign bureaus.

It was also during O'Neil's reign that host and producer Robert-Guy Scully was hired in 1983. In 1977, he had generated some controversy by making what many felt to be contemptuous remarks regarding Quebec at a conference in the United States. Later on, he was in the headlines several times after not informing CBC/Radio-Canada about some of the financial sources[17] of several of his company's productions, such the Canadian Heritage Minutes, *Le Canada du millénaire*, and the film *Maurice Richard*. Part of the financing had come from a federal government agency, the Canada Information Office, created to promote Canadian unity. The funds were channelled through the sponsorship of big companies like Via Rail or BCE, which served as intermediaries to shield the source of the money. The Chrétien government had found a discreet and astute way to intervene directly in Radio-Canada programs. Scully testified at the Gomery Commission inquiry into the sponsorship scandal.

Fortunately for us, at the time O'Neil was also hiring editorial managers with a solid journalistic background, particularly Claude Saint-Laurent, who came from *La Presse*, and Marcel Desjardins, from *Montréal-Matin*.

It is not hard to imagine how much all this Liberal activity in News and Current Affairs was irritating the Progressive Conservatives, including Minister Marcel Masse. The Liberals stood accused of acting as if they owned Radio-Canada. This was the time when Brian Mulroney and the PCs were trying to rally the entire country around an agreement to recognize a "distinct society" in Quebec, the famous Meech Lake Accord, which was fiercely opposed by the Liberals.

In 1991, Pierre O'Neil officially retired. In fact, he was fired, along with two other senior managers, for reasons that have never really been explained. Perhaps the vice-president, Guy Gougeon, simply wanted to clean house. Whatever the reason, the decision was made near the end of Brian Mulroney's second mandate. Here is an excerpt from an article by Louise Cousineau from the September 17, 1991, edition of *La Presse*:

Three big bosses fired at Radio-Canada.... We have never seen so many heads roll at once at Radio-Canada. The Managing Director of General Television and the Director of Television News and Current Affairs have been fired. Andréanne Bournival and Pierre O'Neil will leave their positions on Friday of this week. The Managing Director of Sales, Pierre Vachon, is also out.

So Pierre O'Neil was gone and Marcel Masse had been able to get his new act adopted, but there was still a reference to the defence of national unity, a remnant of the old act still listed in the CBC's Journalistic Standards and Practices. Many journalists had wanted to see the disappearance of this reminder of an era that they hoped was finally over.

Jean-François Lépine was among them, which is probably why he missed out in the close race to replace Pierre O'Neil as head of News and Current Affairs.

As the preferred candidate of both Gérard Veilleux, the president of CBC/Radio-Canada, and Guy Gougeon, the vice-president of French Television, to succeed O'Neil, Lépine had been invited to apply for the position. He had indicated that he would accept it only on the condition that the famous reference to the promotion of national unity be struck from the preamble to the CBC's Journalistic Standards and Practices. He had even denounced this text publicly at a University of Ottawa conference some time previously.

During his last meeting with the selection committee, he insisted once again on this condition. The committee included four people: Trina McQueen from the English network, executive recruiter Jean-Pierre Bourbonnais, VP of French Television Guy Gougeon, and the editor-in-chief of *Le Devoir*, Lise Bissonnette. McQueen asked Lépine to answer the following question clearly: "Yes or no, if the reference to national unity is not struck, are you a candidate?" He answered: "No!" At forty years of age, Jean-François Lépine had just lost his opportunity to become the head of News and Current Affairs at Radio-Canada.[18]

Ironically, in the course of the following year, the standards were adapted to the new Broadcasting Act and the reference was struck.

Waves of Cutbacks

If Marcel Masse was able to contribute to the clarification of the law, his government did not hesitate to cut CBC/Radio-Canada down to size. We worry a lot about the independence of the public broadcaster, but in fact its direction is often most influenced by budget cuts. When he first came into power in 1984, Brian Mulroney had handed over responsibility for closely reviewing all government programs to his deputy prime minister, Erik Nielsen. This included CBC/Radio-Canada's budget.

It's fair to say that everyone was becoming aware of budgetary deficits and the quickly increasing level of public debt. It had to be slowed down, and CBC/Radio-Canada would not be spared, even if the deficits grew under the Mulroney government. So it was that in 1985, a year after I had started at Radio-Canada, the employees' concern for their future was at its height. The Conservative budget included major cuts. The government was slashing $85 million from CBC/Radio-Canada's parliamentary allocation, which translated into 1,150 job cuts across the country. It was only the beginning of a long cycle of budget cuts. For Marcel Masse, it was nevertheless an opportunity to define the role and mandate of CBC/Radio-Canada. This would lead to major discussions with Pierre Juneau. Masse explained:

> If we have created a public institution, it is because we have given it specific responsibilities, certainly not to compete with the private sector. If CBC/Radio-Canada keeps advertising, it will die.… But then, CBC/Radio-Canada wanted more money. But it wasn't money that was needed; it was to return to its original mandate as a public institution. I told Juneau, "If we take away advertising, you will be able to raise the bar for culture. In return, we could give all the advertising room over to the private broadcasters."[19]

Masse then proposed his solution to the president of CBC/Radio-Canada:

> We could tax advertising and put the proceeds in your
> "budget" and from there we could adjust things as we
> went along. So that was something that Pierre Juneau
> and I discussed. It was my option and it continues to be
> an option today. [20]

It was not the option that won the day. Instead, the trend was to be
pragmatic about budget cuts. CBC/Radio-Canada management opted
then, as it continues to do today, to counter the budget cuts by seeking out more revenue streams. These came primarily from advertising,
which grew from 17 percent of the total budget in 1982 to 28 percent in
1989. This growth continued, reaching 36 percent of the total budget by
2012–2013.

As many people had warned, this search for commercial revenues
to compensate for the reduction of the parliamentary grant increased
the pressure to produce programs that would generate more advertising
revenues. This meant that Radio-Canada had to give over many hours a
day to the same kind of programming as its "competitor from across the
street," the private TVA.

In the long run, these decisions played into the hands of those who
argued that there was no longer a need for a public broadcaster like CBC/
Radio-Canada. I am not saying here that programming should be elitist.
For example, in News and Current Affairs, I had always defended the
idea that all subjects of public interest should be covered, whether this
meant general local news or major international events. But they had to
be covered our way, the way a public service does it, with all the subtle-
ties, precautions, and perspective required.

At the start of his mandate, in 1985, Marcel Masse had hoped for
a major rethink. He charged Florian Sauvageau and Gerald Caplan[21]
with the task of analyzing the whole Canadian audiovisual system
and redefining the role of CBC/Radio-Canada from there. Sauvageau
remembers the context:

> It is interesting that Masse chose to create his own task
> force. It was necessary to review the Broadcasting Act.

The advent of cable television had changed everything, the specialty channels were growing and many conservatives did not like CBC/Radio-Canada. But Masse knew that I was a defender of the public broadcaster. He had promised me that he would not interfere with our work, and he kept that promise. [22]

In fact, the Caplan-Sauvageau report,[23] published in 1986, was very useful in providing a better understanding of the audiovisual environment. It painted an accurate portrait of the competitive environment and the new players, the specialty channels, who were coming into a universe that had been dominated to that point by general television networks. It gave Minister Masse several compelling arguments to shape the future Broadcasting Act of 1991. For example, Caplan and Sauvageau wanted the broadcasters to offer more Canadian content, notably through CRTC regulation to ensure that private networks would spend more on Canadian programs. The report proposed the creation of a second public network (CBC/Radio-Canada 2) and, above all, stressed that public television be better funded. Finally, the report recommended a change to the appointment process for members of CBC/Radio-Canada's board.[24]

Florian Sauvageau remains very proud of the report:

> I realize that I am not objective on the subject, but I think that our report had an impact. The 1991 Broadcasting Act recognized the differences between the English- and French-language systems; that was very important for me. It also established a place for community media, equal to the public and private sectors; I cared about that too.... And the mandate to contribute to national unity was changed. That's something, at least!
>
> Of course, Radio-Canada continued to decline (under all the parties), but that has nothing to do with the Broadcasting Act. That's a political story![25]

Caplan and Sauvageau's thoughts on the place of the public broadcaster, its role, and its mandate did not lead to the extensive debate that they had hoped to stimulate. In the meantime, senior management at CBC/Radio-Canada continued to downsize in lockstep with successive budget cuts. These were certainly not the ideal conditions in which to prepare for an entirely new media environment, with specialty channels, the growing power of cable distributors, and the hostility of private broadcasters. Pragmatism in the management of public service has its limits.

In 1990, Brian Mulroney's dream of reintegrating Quebec into the Canadian constitution "with honour and enthusiasm" did not achieve unanimity — far from it. The famous Meech Lake Accord, which would have given Quebec the status of a distinct society within Canada, failed. In Quebec City, Premier Bourassa said at the time,

> English Canada must understand clearly that, whatever
> is said and whatever is done, Quebec is, today and always,
> a distinct society, free and capable of assuming responsi-
> bility for its own destiny and its own development.

Two years later, on October 26, 1992, in a final attempt to save the day, the government held a referendum that is nearly forgotten today, seeking approval of the Charlottetown Accord setting out a new constitutional arrangement. This apparently satisfied no one. A few months after this second failure, Brian Mulroney resigned from office.

Then, on November 4, 1993, Jean Chrétien and the Liberal Party returned to power after nine years of Progressive Conservative government. And on September 26, 1994, with the election of Jacques Parizeau and the Parti Québécois, Quebec and Canada entered into an era of renewed tensions. The country appeared to be truly on the verge of a rupture.

While the great political struggle of the 1995 referendum was in gestation, Radio-Canada was once again going through a financial crisis. The president, Anthony Manera, who had only assumed the office in February 1994, resigned with great fanfare on February 27, 1995, declaring that "CBC/Radio-Canada will not be able to fulfill its mandate adequately" and that he did not want to "preside over the dismantling"[26] of the public broadcaster.

Tony Manera had been the vice-president of human resources at CBC/Radio-Canada for ten years before being named president. He was astounded that the Liberal government had announced much deeper cuts in its budget than the minister of Canadian heritage, Michel Dupuy, had led him to expect.

Paul Racine was assistant deputy minister of Canadian heritage at the time. He had discussed the forthcoming cuts in CBC/Radio-Canada's funding with Manera. According to him, "Minister Dupuy was not able to decide. So the Treasury Board made the cuts, and Dupuy always said he had not taken the decision and that he had not been consulted."[27]

Racine holds the view that of all the ministers of communications and heritage with whom he had worked — he knew eight of them — Michel Dupuy was the weakest and Marcel Masse the strongest:

> [Marcel Masse] always had Brian Mulroney's ear. And he had an exceptional quality, he could sometimes even go and get new money for his department. In addition, we were experiencing a period of extraordinary collaboration with the province of Quebec. It was a great period of co-operation. There were much fewer tensions than before. During the two Mulroney mandates [1984–1993], I never felt resentment toward Radio-Canada, while the Liberals always fed these tensions.[28]

Pierre Juneau's Helping Hand

To replace Tony Manera, Jean Chrétien appointed Perrin Beatty, a former Progressive Conservative minister, as president of CBC/Radio-Canada. This time, the prime minister could certainly not be accused of putting a partisan Liberal in the job. Perhaps to calm things down after Tony Manera's surprise resignation, the government set up a committee mandated by the Department of Supply and Services to examine the mandates of CBC/Radio-Canada, the NFB, and Telefilm Canada. The committee was chaired by Pierre Juneau, who was no pushover. In January 1996, his report concluded that CBC/Radio-Canada should be given the means to get out of its impasse. The report was titled *Making our Voices Heard: Canadian Broadcasting and Film for the 21st Century.*

It proposed a new tax on cable distributors to meet the needs of CBC/Radio-Canada: "It's a tax on cable companies, not on consumers. It would represent an increase of $1.50 per month for the average subscriber."

At the same time, it was very critical of Radio-Canada television, which had become "a hybrid, a television enterprise which was neither a real business nor a true public service." Marcel Masse must have smiled on reading this in the report.

Juneau's report therefore recommended that CBC/Radio-Canada stop chasing ratings and advertisers entirely.

These were audacious conclusions. At the time, I was president of la Fédération professionnelle des journalistes du Québec, the professional association for journalists in the province, and we welcomed the report:

> The FPJQ recognizes that the financing model proposed, a new tax, risks being vigorously opposed. But for the FPJQ, the "Juneau version" of CBC/Radio-Canada would be worth the cost. This financing model would guarantee a certain freedom from the influence of advertisers, but it would also guarantee the Corporation's independence from the political power of the day, which has been mishandled recently by the Chrétien government.[29]

The opposition to the Juneau report was scathing.

The proposed cable tax recommendation was leaked, which allowed the industry to orchestrate a solid lobbying and public relations campaign to strike down the idea the minute the report appeared. Not surprisingly, since the cable companies would have had to contribute to CBC/Radio-Canada's financing.

Lise Bissonnette, then editor-in-chief of *Le Devoir*, wrote, "It would be unfortunate if the debate on financing, which promises to be stormy, were to derail such a great proposal."[30]

The great proposal never garnered enough support to reach the stage of any kind of real discussion. It was another missed opportunity in the history of the public broadcaster.

Precisely because it is important to emphasize Pierre Juneau's contribution to the debate about the public broadcaster, we will give him the last word here. The same man the sovereigntists suspected of trying to push the organization into producing federalist propaganda in his time as president of CBC/Radio-Canada (1982–1989), in fact, demonstrated that he had a great sense of public service. In February 1996, he spoke out against the position taken by the new minister of Canadian heritage, Sheila Copps: "Culture and politics are better left apart. CBC/Radio-Canada must be open, but not to broadcast propaganda for anyone."[31]

That statement must have brought a smile to the face of the former Progressive Conservative minister of communications, Marcel Masse.

CHAPTER 7

From One Referendum to Another

The Charlottetown referendum of 1992 seems to have been forgotten. Nonetheless, it led to the usual kind of ideological battles between sovereigntists and federalists. In this tense climate, management decided to make major changes to the French network's flagship daily public affairs show, *Le Point*, where I worked at the time. Journalist Jean Pelletier was the program's new editor-in-chief; Louis Lalande (subsequently vice-president of the French networks) was the coordinating producer; Jean-François Lépine was the host. Many of the previous season's colleagues had been moved out. I was the studio coordinating producer, a bit removed from the daily management of the show. All these changes had created a heavy atmosphere. Many journalists were not happy that their new boss was the son of the former minister, Gérard Pelletier. It is true that Jean Pelletier shared his father's passion for journalism, but he also shared the same federalist convictions, which he expressed freely. In my experience, in fact, he was one of the rare people, whether working journalists or managers, to have expressed political convictions so freely in the presence of other employees. (As I said earlier, I believe it is preferable to keep one's political opinions to oneself when exercising editorial responsibilities at Radio-Canada.) However, I always acknowledged that Jean Pelletier had excellent journalistic instincts and was very cultivated. When I joined management myself in 2006, I took great pleasure in developing a close professional relationship with him, particularly with regard to the supervision of the investigative journalism program *Enquêtes*, for which he had responsibility.

But in 1992, this morose environment at *Le Point*, in conjunction with a very well remunerated offer from Quebec's educational television network, Radio-Québec, influenced my decision to leave Radio-Canada for what turned out to be two years. I felt the need for a change and a chance to get more management experience under my belt. At Radio-Québec, I oversaw several programs, including *Droit de parole* (*The Right to Speak*), *Québec Magazine*, and *Le Choc du présent* (*The Shock of the Present*).

I have always been drawn to current affairs. A program such as *Droit de parole*, when it features the right subject matter and the right guests, offers an extraordinary platform to debate ideas. This type of program has almost disappeared from the radar of Radio-Canada's main television network, as if face-to-face debates of ideas were old-fashioned, banished, since they have been labelled *shows de chaises*, literally "chair shows," or, in English, talking heads. This is unfortunate, as we have lost something valuable in the process.

I am not suggesting we should return to the beginnings of television. Of course it is important to present modern television, reports on the ground, and to show events as they are unfolding. As a producer, I had produced many such reports at home and abroad.

However that may be, my time at Radio-Québec gave me experience in managing teams, up until my return as a producer on Radio-Canada's *Enjeux* (*The Stakes*) in 1995, the year when another, much more meaningful, referendum would take place.

RDI, the Great New Thing

On January 1, 1995, Radio-Canada's new all-news channel, le Réseau de l'information (RDI), launched its programming. The new network was part of the legacy of Claude Saint-Laurent, who had succeeded Pierre O'Neil as head of television News and Current Affairs in 1991. Saint-Laurent had fought hard, even internally, to convince everyone that the project was viable.

Unlike the rest of Radio-Canada's radio and television services, RDI was not financed through a government grant but rather by cable subscriptions. The launch of the new channel was a rare ray of hope to Radio-Canada, which had seen nothing but downsizing over the preceding years.

Mostly, the new network was meeting an essential need. We were entering a time of continuous information flow, and it was out of the question for this country's francophones to rely on American networks such as CNN or on the English network's Newsworld for round-the-clock news.

Under its first director, Renaud Gilbert, RDI dramatically disrupted Radio-Canada's existing journalistic practices. From then on, any news item would hit the air as soon as it became available. The profession as a whole had to get used to the idea of practising journalism entirely differently. There were no more deadlines, since RDI could easily make the front page of the newspaper obsolete. The new network was strongly criticized — sometimes rightly, when it elevated something insignificant to prominence, and sometimes unjustly, by the competition, whose habits and work schedules were being rudely disrupted.

At the launch of RDI's programming, on New Year's Day 1995, as president of the FPJQ, I welcomed the new media outlet enthusiastically, but I also understood that from now on, the news cycle would speed up tremendously.

We were at the start of a very intense time for news. Jean Chrétien was prime minister, and the leader of the Official Opposition of Canada was Lucien Bouchard, a sovereigntist from the Bloc Québécois. A leader of the Official Opposition who wanted to take Quebec out of Canada was something that the country had never seen before! Then, in September 1994, Jacques Parizeau and the Parti Québécois took power in Quebec with the avowed objective of holding a referendum on sovereignty. The collision of identities between sovereigntists and federalists was occurring again, and RDI was debuting just in time to do the play-by-play in this political war.

"It was the 1995 referendum that really launched RDI," says Renaud Gilbert.[1] The closer we got to October 30, referendum day, the more the network was attacked, as much by the sovereigntists as the federalists. Both sides accused it of bias. The federalist side used the expression "RD-Oui," a play on words implying that the network was over-promoting the "yes" or sovereigntist cause, while the sovereigntist side called the channel "Radio-Ô-Canada" … which is self-explanatory! The major difference, however, is that as the party responsible for the public broadcaster, the Government of Canada felt more entitled to criticize it, adopting the entitled attitude of an owner. To a lesser degree, it was not unusual to hear some of the prominent voices in the sovereigntist camp raised to accuse Radio-Canada of broadcasting federalist propaganda in Quebec.

Radio-Canada and all of its components were in the sights of all the political players because of its prominence in its traditional role of provider of political news and current affairs. 1995 was no exception to the rule.

The Big Love-in

One event in particular brought the tension over the referendum campaign to a head and revealed the level of pressure on journalists, particularly those from Radio-Canada. On October 27, 1995, three days before the referendum, the most important question was: how many people had been at the famous federalist love-in at Place du Canada in Montreal, where thousands of citizens from across the country had gathered to express their attachment to Quebec? The federalist side accused Quebec journalists — especially those from Radio-Canada — of having underestimated the size of the crowd.

Let's open a parenthesis here.

Historically, the media have always had trouble estimating the size of large crowds at public demonstrations. For example, there have been epic quarrels among the parade organizers on occasions such as the Fête nationale (Quebec's official holiday), St. Patrick's Day, Canada Day, and other big rallies, each of them claiming to hold the historical record for attendance. The symbolism of numbers is a big deal in political contests. As president of the FPJQ, I intervened several times in the early 1990s to call on the media to be more rigorous when evaluating the size of crowds. Among other ideas, I had proposed that the media use independent experts to estimate the size of crowds at large public events. I welcomed an initiative at La Presse, which had retained an independent firm to evaluate the number of people at the Fête nationale and at Canada Day festivities in 1992: "Such an initiative fills a major gap in the world of news. I would like to take this opportunity to encourage other media outlets to adopt this initiative."[2]

End of parenthesis.

On October 27, 1995, crowd estimates for the largest "no" side rally in Montreal were the subject of an incredible ideological war. Radio-Canada's journalists were accused of every sin under the sun.

A report on the 1995 referendum coverage prepared by Donna Logan at the request of the CBC/Radio-Canada board discusses the issue of the controversial crowd estimates of the "no" rally:

> The size of the crowd assembled for the occasion was another subject of controversy.... Evaluations of the number of participants at the rally in Dominion Square varied between 35,000 and 150,000 or more. Signing off at the end of a special he was anchoring on RDI, Jean Bédard[3] asserted that official police sources had counted the crowd at 35,000. In introducing Jean Charest, Lisa Frulla[4] said: "According to the helicopters [sic] we are more than 150,000 here today." ... On Newsworld, co-anchors Don Newman and Alison Smith said as they began their live coverage that the wire services estimated the crowd at 150,000.[5]

As always during these ideological duels, the francophone reporters were much more closely watched than their anglophone counterparts. In the CBC coverage of the Montreal love-in, Mike Duffy reported from the crowd wearing a tie with a red maple leaf while seemingly oblivious to any sense of conflict of interest. The francophone reporters, wherever their private sympathies might lie, would never have gotten away with showing their colours in the same way — whether it was the maple leaf or the fleur-de-lys. Claude Saint-Laurent remembers how difficult it was to cope with all the accusations of bias thrown at Radio-Canada in the wake of this event:

Pierre Jomphe[6] and I came up with the great idea of shutting up all the critics by calling on scientific expertise to evaluate the exact number of people in the huge crowd. We asked land surveyors to use aerial photographs to establish the area involved.[7]

Here is how the day unfolded: on the air, Jean Bédard estimated the crowd at 35,000. He was drawing on a range of sources, from police to reporters on the ground, including traffic reporter Roger Laroche, who was watching from Radio-Canada's small plane, the *Vol-au-vent*. The number had not been plucked out of thin air, as the police had already provided advance estimates of the number of people that would fit into the available space.

After Jean Bédard's on-air estimate, the "no" camp sent out a statement on the Telbec wire (Release #300,095, dated October 27, 1995, at 3:21:58 p.m.) headlined "More than 40,000 Québécois and Canadians Express Their Pride."

Then, thirty minutes later, a dramatic update from the "no" forces: "The preceding release contained an error (Ref. Telbec message #300,095, 16:03:34). More than 100,000 Québécois and Canadians Express Their Pride."[8]

From the stage at Place du Canada, host Liza Frulla went even further. "There are 150,000 of us here!" declared the vice-president of the "no" forces. Today, Frulla smiles when she is reminded of the event. "On stage, someone whispered to me that we were 150,000 people. It was a beautiful number, so I repeated it at the microphone. But no matter what, it was one of the largest demonstrations I had ever seen."[9]

All the same, this jump in the estimate from 35,000 to 150,000 was surprising — especially since the "no" committee and the Quebec Liberal Party had stated in advance that the space could only contain between 35,000 and 38,000 people.

But the harm was done. Radio-Canada's journalists were accused of conspiring with the separatists in the "yes" camp. The *Toronto Star*'s Rosie DiManno was among those to write in this vein.

These were the reasons why the head of News and Current Affairs,

Claude Saint-Laurent, and his colleague Pierre Jomphe wanted to counter the accusations of partisanship by retaining scientific experts. Their conclusion: there were at most 39,500 people, with a margin of error of 25 percent! Radio-Canada was comfortably within the zone of accuracy. "In the end, we have an irreproachable crowd estimate! We were very proud of it!" remembers Saint-Laurent.[10]

Days after the close "no" victory, Jean Chrétien did not hesitate to accuse Radio-Canada of siding with the sovereigntist camp: "Radio-Canada has a mandate to promote national unity, but this was obviously not among its preoccupations night after night when I was watching."[11] Four years after the Progressive Conservatives had adopted a new law, Chrétien showed that he neither understood nor accepted that Radio-Canada no longer had a legal mandate to "contribute to the development of national unity." He was purposely ignoring the 1991 Broadcasting Act and referring instead to the 1968 version, adopted under the Pearson government. The fact that Chrétien was once again referring to it showed that the 1968 wording remained very meaningful for the Liberals.

The president of CBC/Radio-Canada, Perrin Beatty, "distanced himself timidly from Jean Chrétien's statement",[12] reported the headline in Le Devoir. The Globe and Mail was more generous towards him: "Beatty Reminds PM That Networks Are Public, Not State, Broadcasters."[13]

Be that as it may, Claude Saint-Laurent had thumbed his nose at those who criticized the work of his journalists. His experts' crowd estimate also allowed him to cut off accusations that were even coming from some members of CBC/Radio-Canada's board. The board had given Donna Logan a mandate to chair a committee called Media Responsibility to evaluate the coverage of the corporation's English- and French-language News and Current Affairs. The committee had in turn commissioned an independent study from Toronto-based Erin Research. Their report, prepared a few weeks after the referendum, concluded that from a political standpoint, the coverage was fair and balanced on both networks.

The conclusion to this incident: the only promotion that Radio-Canada's journalists should be doing was of free and independent news and current affairs that respected the basic rules of the profession. And whether one favoured Quebec sovereignty or Canadian federalism, the changes made by Marcel Masse certainly provided the public broadcaster's journalists with more freedom to do their jobs and more credibility in the eyes of the public.

Jean Chrétien's Response

The prime minister's conclusion was quite different. His reaction was scathing. It was in the time immediately after the 1995 referendum that CBC/Radio-Canada had to absorb the most spectacular cut to its budget ever.

A graphic prepared by Friends of Canadian Broadcasting, reproduced with permission here, tells the story.[14] The amounts indicated cover the overall parliamentary grant for both English and French networks.

The numbers in this graphic describe the total amount allocated to both English and French networks. The table differentiates between two types of grants; some amounts are designated to the operating budget (grey line), while the black line covers all types of funding, including the amounts reserved for building maintenance and development of infrastructure. The production funding mentioned at the bottom of the graphic refers to amounts allocated to independent producers who sell their programs to broadcasters. These funds are also available to private broadcasters as part of Canada's hybrid public-private broadcasting system.

The dramatic budget cuts inflicted by the Chrétien government began in 1994–1995 and continued until 1998–1999.

Robert Rabinovitch knew the CBC/Radio-Canada file well. Before becoming its president in 1999, he had been a senior bureaucrat in the Government of Canada from 1968 to 1986, notably as deputy minister of communications from 1982 to 1985. He had therefore known the corporation for a long time. The former president adds this to the picture:

> If the table had started in the 1970s I think you would find that there has been no real increase in the CBC/ SRC budget since 1976 and we all know what happened in 1976 including PET's statement that he would subject it to a "mise en tutelle" [put it in trusteeship] SRC if it

Change in Parliamentary Appropriation to the CBC
(in 2014 $)

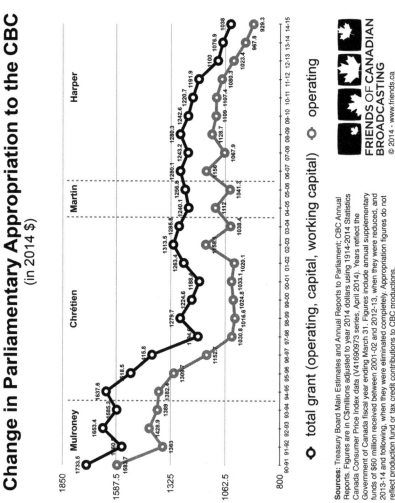

○ total grant (operating, capital, working capital)   ◇ operating

FRIENDS OF CANADIAN
BROADCASTING
© 2014 - www.friends.ca

Sources: Treasury Board Main Estimates and Annual Reports to Parliament; CBC Annual Reports. Figures are in C$millions adjusted to year 2014 dollars using 1914-2014 Statistics Canada Consumer Price Index data (V41690973 series, April 2014). Years reflect the Government of Canada fiscal year ending March 31. Figures include annual supplementary funds of $60 million received between 2001-02 and 2012-13, when they were reduced, and 2013-14 and following, when they were eliminated completely. Appropriation figures do not reflect production fund or tax credit contributions to CBC productions.

did not clean up its sovereigntist act. Suffice it to say all governments have had the same policy of slowly bleeding the CBC/SRC to death. At first we did not fight back and absorbed the cuts. But today it is impossible to get any more water out of the stone without having an effect on content. The one exception to all this was the $60m we received for programming in the 2000s and even that was over Chrétien's dead body.[15]

This pretty much sums up CBC/Radio-Canada's financial history in recent decades, up to the arrival of the current president, Hubert T. Lacroix. As Robert Rabinovitch emphasizes, in order to see the full picture, you would have to go back to earlier years when Trudeau tried to cut Radio-Canada down to size for allowing too much airtime, in his opinion, for "separatist discourse."

The political fights of those years had left their mark. Under Brian Mulroney's Progressive Conservative government, the cuts were smaller than those that followed from 1994 on. In fact, it is important to recognize the impact of decisions made by Jean Chrétien's Liberal government on CBC/Radio-Canada. The only exception was when Rabinovitch succeeded in obtaining an additional $60 million, which had to be renegotiated every year — a financial arrangement obtained through the mediation of deputy ministers and discovered after the fact by Jean Chrétien.

Among governments before Stephen Harper's, the Chrétien regime is the one that most damaged the public broadcaster. Its determination to reverse the federal deficit left victims in its trail. Between 1995 and 2000, the cuts reached $400 million.

The drop was so brutal that in 1997, in an unprecedented gesture of alarm (especially given the diverse relationships among them) four former presidents of CBC/Radio-Canada — Al Johnson, Pierre Juneau, Tony Manera, and Laurent Picard — signed a joint letter:

> Since 1985, the CBC has lost 38 per cent of the purchasing power of its parliamentary allocation...." Canada

spends far less on public broadcasting than most other developed countries: $32 per capita per year,[16] to serve a huge, diverse, bilingual, and multicultural country. Belgium, which is also bilingual, spends $58, the United Kingdom spends $60, Japan $56, and Switzerland $109.[17]

This intervention by the former presidents was warmly received by CBC/Radio-Canada employees and management, particularly because the letter underlined a perverse consequence of the large budget cuts:

> This revenue gap has forced the CBC to solicit ever more advertising to fund its television networks, introducing an inevitable and growing distortion of its programming decisions.[18]

Ever since, close observers have rightly concluded that the public broadcaster's independence is far more threatened by direct budget cuts than by the odd political interference in its programming. Is cutting off the lifeline not the most effective intervention of all? The head of French News and Current Affairs from 1991 to 2003, Claude Saint-Laurent, says with conviction, "There was never anyone in twelve years who interfered directly or indirectly, from the provincial or federal governments, in my decisions about managing the News and Current Affairs department."[19]

Of course he admits that at times there were very tough criticisms levelled at Radio-Canada — for example, during the 1995 referendum — but "never direct or indirect interventions or pressure on me." However, he lived through budget cuts under two governments, Progressive Conservative and Liberal. "I was Managing Director of News and Current Affairs for twelve years, and no government over those years spared Radio-Canada!"[20]

The best way to influence Radio-Canada is to reduce its government funding and to remind it, every year, that the politicians hold the chequebook. Jean Chrétien's Liberal government used this power freely — which is what caused Pierre Gravel, an editorial writer at *La Presse*, to write:

All Canadian Prime Ministers have undoubtedly dreamt about it. In any case, in his time, Brian Mulroney would have loved to have President Pierre Juneau's head on a platter. And before him, Pierre Trudeau, who threatened to shut the whole place down and to show nothing but Chinese vases on television. But in the end, it may be Jean Chrétien who will succeed. Nothing seems to stop Ottawa in its latest offensive to increase its ability to put pressure on the public broadcaster's orientation.[21]

In April 1999, Ian Morrison, spokesperson for Friends of Canadian Broadcasting, said, "I think we have reason to believe that Jean Chrétien is the most hostile Prime Minister to the CBC since its creation by Mackenzie King in 1936."[22]

It is worth noting a brief incident that happened on the English network under the Chrétien government.

During the summit meeting of the Asia-Pacific Economic Cooperation Forum (APEC) in Vancouver in 1997, Jean Chrétien's director of communications, Peter Donolo, took CBC reporter Terry Milewski to task. In an official complaint, he accused Milewski of biased coverage and of having taken the side of demonstrators at the conference. It is extremely rare in the history of CBC/Radio-Canada for an official complaint to come directly from the Prime Minister's Office (PMO). Donolo reproached Milewski for having exchanged emails with the demonstrators, who were denouncing the arrival in Vancouver of Haji Mohammed Suharto, the Indonesian dictator. The police had generously "seasoned" the demonstrators with cayenne pepper. The "Peppergate Affair" as we called it, took months to wend its way to a conclusion.

Finally, in 1999, the ombudsman of the French network, Marcel Pépin, who had inherited the file, responded to the complaint:

Finally the role, even the mandate of the Director of Communications in the Prime Minister's Office is to ensure that the PM's message, on any subject, attracts the attention of the media and that it be covered the way his services want to see it covered. In the case before us here it is the PMO, therefore the Prime Minister himself, we must conclude, who did not like the way CBC reporter Terry Milewski covered the APEC summit, as well as the security measures taken at the time and the consequences that have followed since then.[23]

Having provided a lesson in journalism and an explanation of what constitutes a free and independent news media, the ombudsman absolved the reporter.

The Red Carpet for Advertising

In 1997–1998, managing Radio-Canada had become untenable. The situation was such that we cannot reproach management with not having tried everything to save the day. The people in charge of programming skilfully tried to reconcile the public service mandate with the budget cuts. Mission impossible, some will say.

McKinsey, the famous management consulting firm, was asked to take a close look at CBC/Radio-Canada's finances and management. The upshot was that regional stations would be affected — some shut down — and hundreds of employees packed off to retirement. What choice did management have to fill the continuing funding gap? They kept gravitating, inevitably, to the search for more advertising revenues, just as the former presidents of CBC/Radio-Canada had predicted in 1997.

This had led Johnson, Juneau, Manera, and Picard to conclude,

> We consider that it is crucial for Canada that the government return to its own philosophy of recognizing that culture is more important than ever in Canada, and of the central role of a well established and adequately financed CBC/Radio-Canada. The first step in this direction would be to cancel the additional budget cuts scheduled for 1997 and 1998. [24]

The Robert Rabinovitch Presidency

It was in this morose climate that I entered the management of Radio-Canada's Radio News service in February 1997. As a journalist and a producer, I had often criticized management. The challenge was to do better. I never regretted my decision. I had the good fortune to share my passion for public service with great people, both employees and fellow managers.

In 1999, the vice-president of French Radio, Sylvain Lafrance, offered me the position of managing director of News and Current Affairs in French Radio. That same year, Robert Rabinovitch became president and CEO of CBC/Radio-Canada.

Rabinovitch was passionate about public service and loved Montreal, which he never missed an opportunity to demonstrate. He is of superior intellect: a cultured, determined, and unpretentious man. His face is always expressive, and he always seems to be reflecting, evaluating the situation he's in or the people he meets. When he discusses something with you, he never looks away. And as a bonus, he has a great sense of humour.

Rabinovitch is a sophisticated observer of both the world of communications and the machinery of government. He has always defined himself as a public servant. With regard to CBC/Radio-Canada, he has always insisted on its independence. For him, the public broadcaster is a public service, not a state broadcaster. In other words, public broadcasting must neither serve the government of the day nor spread state propaganda. Still, Jean Chrétien is the one who appointed him president of CBC/Radio-Canada. Rabinovitch says the prime minister thought he was fearless to have accepted the position. But the new president was proud to join a great institution.

The appointment was well received. In his editorial of October 20, 1999, Mario Roy of *La Presse* saluted the arrival of Rabinovitch and wrote, "… if we know that he is close to the federal Liberals, he is also said to have a great independence of spirit, which would indicate that he is up to the job of resisting political pressure…."[25]

Mario Roy saw clearly what I later witnessed for myself. Throughout his mandate as president, I often spent time with Robert Rabinovitch.

During this period, I was in the position of director of Radio News and Current Affairs, then managing director of News and Current Affairs, all platforms for the French services. There was never any pressure from him. Better still, I constantly heard him reminding everyone of the importance of the arm's-length relationship between Radio-Canada and the government of the day.

In an interview for the October 19, 1999, edition of the *Toronto Star*, the new president said,

> Let's be frank: at the end of the day, if the government and the regulator [the CRTC] want to kill CBC/SRC, it will be killed. My job is to try and give them a good reason not to kill CBC. [26]

This former deputy minister of communications under Pierre Trudeau knew the Ottawa political world well, and he was a friend of Jean Chrétien's closest advisor and chief of staff, Eddie Goldenberg. He could also draw on his vast experience in the senior ranks of the civil service, which had instilled in him the idea of public service as being incompatible with the very idea of partisanship. [27]

The October 19, 1999, *Toronto Star* article added, "He's the quintessential public servant who has managed some of the trickiest folios in government." [28]

In fact, Rabinovitch always made sure that he kept the arm's-length relationship between the government of the day and CBC/Radio-Canada:

> I never discussed programming with the PMO, nor the minister responsible for the CBC, and most were respectful enough not to raise programming issues should I see them at an event. I did, however, consider it appropriate to lobby for board members although most of that was done by the chair. [29]

Before his appointment, Rabinovitch's independent disposition had even led him to join Friends of Canadian Broadcasting's Advisory

Council at a time when the broadcast watchdog was highly critical of the Liberal government's decisions.

Throughout his years as president, Robert Rabinovitch regularly put on sessions to train CBC board members on the independence of the public service.

He often referred to materials prepared by Pierre Trudel, professor in the faculty of law at l'Université de Montréal. For the board meeting held on January 26, 2006, Pierre Nollet, vice-president and secretary to the board, circulated a presentation titled *CBC and the Arm's Length Relationship*.

The document stressed the role of the board members: "It is the board of directors that, in law, embodies and guarantees the protection of the public broadcasters' independence."[30]

The document reminded the reader that this arm's-length relationship is directly inspired by the BBC Charter. It stated that this distance is a fundamental principle linked to freedom of expression and the country's democratic traditions; that the bar must be high for a public broadcaster; and that the corporation serves citizens, not the government.

Another document addressed to the board, titled *CBC/Société Radio-Canada and the Arm's Length Relationship*, prepared by Edith Cody-Rice,[31] discussed public broadcasting principles by quoting the Caplan-Sauvageau report on the subject: "… there remains a fundamental distinction: this is public broadcasting, not state or government propaganda."[32] And further on it states,

> … the public broadcaster has an important privilege without which the notion of service to the public would be altered beyond recognition: that is, freedom from control by vested interests, whether political or financial. This privilege clearly includes freedom to express certain opinions, especially journalistic ones, without fear or reprisal from politicians who would rather not hear themselves or their party taken to task for bad policies or acts of mischief.[33]

Finally, the document referred to the 1932 act that had created CBC/
Radio-Canada:

> In recommending the formation of CBC/Radio-Canada,
> the parliamentary broadcasting committee advocated
> that the corporation have "substantially the powers
> now enjoyed by the British Broadcasting Corporation".
> Because it was created as a public broadcaster, broad-
> casting in the public interest, the crucial arm's-length
> principle was enshrined as a key characteristic.[34]

Another document, once again prepared by Pierre Trudel, illustrates
the president's constant preoccupation with the issue of independence.
He underlines that even the courts have recognized that CBC/Radio-
Canada is not a creature of government.

In CBC and co. v. R, Mr. Justice Estey mentions,

> the desire by Parliament to establish a national broad-
> casting service free from influences of the political
> world, including perhaps both the executive and legisla-
> tive branches of the government, to the extent that such
> influences might impinge upon the proper functioning
> of such a national broadcasting service.[35]

As a few incidents explained in the following chapters will show,
such useful reminders have had to be addressed to board members on a
regular basis.

CHAPTER 8

From One Government to Another

In 1999, the vice-president of French Radio, Sylvain Lafrance, introduced the members of his management team to the new president, Robert Rabinovitch. When it was my turn to speak, he emphasized the fact that as former president of the FPJQ, I had overseen the adoption of a code of ethics for the journalistic profession in Quebec.

This appeared to reassure the new president.

From my first contact with Robert Rabinovitch, he made a good impression on me. In my first exchanges with him, he had insisted on my total independence as managing director of French News and Current Affairs, specifying that he trusted me in the events that were to follow. I can testify that he always respected this principle throughout his presidency.

Radio-Canada's journalists did not get to know this endearing man. Unfortunately, they have mostly retained the memory of difficult labour relations during his term of office, which was marred by a lockout of the technicians' union (STARF) in 2001 and of the communications union (SCRC) in 2002. This is unfortunate, because he undertook major administrative reforms and had a very high level understanding of his role in the defence of the institution. In that way, he was exemplary.

There are few examples of presidents of CBC/Radio-Canada who have made a point of independence from the government of the day. Most have behaved like civil servants, almost order-takers. For example, Rabinovitch's two immediate predecessors, Gérard Veilleux and Perrin Beatty, barely protested the budget cuts imposed on them.

It is also appropriate to credit Rabinovitch's determination to make CBC/Radio-Canada a place where francophones could work in their own language, including in senior management, a situation that has since deteriorated. "I find you francophones too generous, always giving way to the unilingual anglophones in meetings," he said to me one day as we were leaving a joint meeting with CBC English management.

Allies in the World of Politics

When Robert Rabinovitch first became president of CBC/Radio-Canada, we could still count on a few allies in the Parliament of Canada. Clifford Lincoln (LPC) was one of them. He chaired the Standing Committee on Canadian Heritage in the House of Commons, which also included Liza Frulla (Liberal), Carole-Marie Allard (Liberal), Christiane Gagnon (Bloc Québécois), Wendy Lill (NDP), and Jim Abbott (Canadian Alliance, subsequently Conservative). The committee tabled a report which has, unfortunately, been gathering dust on the shelf ever since. And yet it contained interesting potential solutions for CBC/Radio-Canada. "Among other things, it proposed the concept of cultural sovereignty for Canada, a concept which would have been very innovative in English Canada,"[1] explains Liza Frulla, former minister of Canadian heritage. With regard to CBC/Radio-Canada, the support was unequivocal. We can see this, for example, in the following recommendations:

> 6.1: The Committee recommends that Parliament provide the CBC with increased and stable multi-year funding (3 to 5 years) so that it may adequately fulfill its mandate as expressed in the Broadcasting Act.

> 6.3: The Committee recommends that the CBC deliver a strategic plan, with estimated resource requirements, to Parliament within one year of the tabling of this report on how it would fulfill its public service mandate to: a) deliver local and regional programming; b) meet its

Canadian programming objectives; c) deliver new media programming initiatives.

17.3: The Committee expresses its support for increased funding for efforts to enhance diversity in Canadian broadcasting. The CRTC, the CBC and the Canadian Television Fund should seek ways to ensure that their policies and procedures reflect the need to enhance diversity.[2]

In the year 2000, this was unhoped-for support. Many of us began to dream....

Premonitory Dissidence

Too bad! Once again, nobody inside the government followed up. After the Caplan-Sauvageau and the Juneau reports, yet another report was ignored.

However, there was in the report a premonition of what was to come in the form of the dissenting report of the Canadian Alliance/Reform MP for Kootenay-Columbia, Jim Abbott. Reading it makes it easy to understand why the public broadcaster enjoys so little support from the current Conservative Party, which Jim Abbott subsequently joined.

In his 2003 dissent, the Alliance MP recited his party's manifesto:

The Committee's report may claim that the CBC is essential but the facts do not support the claim....

Given these realities Canadian Alliance is convinced that the time has come to reconsider the importance of CBC television....

We would significantly reduce the CBC operating subsidy by commercialization of CBC television....

Canadian Alliance would consider transferring a portion of the current funding for CBC television to new or existing subsidy or tax credit programs to support Canadians creating content for film and television.[3]

As a very small consolation prize, Abbott proposed maintaining the funding for CBC/Radio-Canada's radio operations.

The same Jim Abbott was appointed in 2006 to the position of parliamentary secretary to the minister of Canadian heritage in the newly elected Conservative government. He was therefore partially responsible for the department then led by Bev Oda.[4] Given the previous positions taken by the Harper government, the choice of Abbott presaged the policies that were to come. Asked at the time about the choice of Abbott as parliamentary secretary, the Prime Minister's Office answered laconically:

> Mr. Abbott is the Parliamentary Secretary, so he has an important role to play, … But we haven't yet decided what role he will play and what file he will be overseeing.[5]

We were reassured.…

My Turn to Play Goalie

Shortly after the 2006 federal election, I was appointed managing director of News and Current Affairs for both radio and television. I had told the staff that I would concentrate on two particular areas during my term in office. First, I wanted to offer more international news on all our platforms. Who else but a public broadcaster, with many experts in the field, can offer this kind of window on the world? In my opinion, it was the best service we could offer to francophones in this country.

I also told them I would focus on investigative journalism. I set up a specialized team in this area, as well as *Enquête*, a weekly program entirely focused on investigative journalism. Among all the things I was able to accomplish at Radio-Canada, I am most proud of this.

The impact of Radio-Canada's investigative journalism has been recognized by the entire profession (and by its critics), particularly by Canadian Journalists for Free Expression, which awarded *Enquête* its Tara Singh Hayer Award in 2012, and by the Fédération professionnelle des journalistes du Québec, which awarded it the Prix Judith-Jasmin in 2014 in recognition of two investigative pieces, one on the Lac Mégantic train derailment and the other on problematic contracts in the construction industry.

Christine St-Pierre's Botched Intervention

The life of a news director is always full of surprises. So it was that on September 7, 2006, I nearly choked on my coffee. Among the letters to the editor in that morning's edition of *La Presse*, my eye was drawn to one supporting Canada's military presence in Afghanistan, the subject of major public discussion at the time:

> Many voices are being raised to demand your return home. I say, please, no.… You are risking your lives there to prevent the terrorist Taliban regime from returning to power. We must not forget the public executions, the hunger, the rapes, the little girls banished from school, the women condemned to wearing the horrible burqa.…[6]

The letter was signed by a Christine St-Pierre.

Was this the same person who was our parliamentary correspondent in Ottawa? The same one whom Radio-Canada had assigned to, among other things, cover defence and foreign affairs?

Yes, it was. It was going to be a very busy day.…

Christine St-Pierre was an experienced journalist. She knew very well that she had just taken a stand on a controversial matter and thereby renounced her ability to cover Canada's military participation in Afghanistan. After suspending her for a day with pay and taking the time to check the facts carefully, I decided to remove her from the parliamentary bureau and to reassign her to other responsibilities. Over the course of the following weeks, she produced a historical document for the series *Tout le monde en parlait* (*Everyone Was Talking About It*) about a 1986 labour conflict at the Manoir Richelieu hotel.

St-Pierre clearly understood the situation. Her gesture — although a botched one — was no doubt part of her personal reflection on her future as a journalist. It is sometimes difficult to reconcile oneself with the duty of neutrality that is part of serving Radio-Canada. Just six months later, I was not surprised to see her launching her political career as a candidate for the Quebec Liberal Party. She was elected on March 26, 2007, and she became minister of culture, communications and the status of women in the Charest government. In April 2014, Premier Philippe Couillard appointed her minister of international relations with responsibility for the Francophonie.

It was during the 2007 election campaign that another reporter, Bernard Drainville, also went into politics as a candidate for the Parti Québécois. Radio-Canada therefore had two reporters running, one Péquiste and one Liberal. At the time, as a running gag, I would go from one office to another in the News Centre, inviting other journalists to hurry up and join the race, ideally for Mario Dumont's Action Démocratique du Québec: "Then I'll be able to say that we reflect all the political parties here at Radio-Canada."

Recently, I discovered that another of our former reporters, Alexandre Lahaie, had become a communications adviser to Chantal Soucy, the member of the national assembly (Coalition Avenir Québec) for Saint-Hyacinthe.

Radio-Canada has often been accused of aligning itself with the separatist movement. I have always found that accusation ridiculous, just as casting the public broadcaster as a faithful spokesman for federalism would be.

I believe that the broadcaster's staff must be made up of journalists and creators from all the different streams of opinion in society and not solely from any particular one. The staff must reflect society as it exists, otherwise there is the risk of distorting reality on the air.

I know very well that Radio-Canada's journalists represent most of the political spectrum. And that is as it should be. The best on-air balance emerges when a diverse range of opinions are debated while preparing the programming.

Radio-Canada's federalist critics always make a big fuss if journalists leave the organization to become candidates for the Parti Québécois. This happened recently with Bernard Drainville,[7] Pierre Duchesne,[8] and Raymond Archambault.[9] But that is forgetting Christine St-Pierre and others, such as program host Robert Desbiens, who was a candidate for the Liberal Party of Canada, or Hélène Narayana, the reporter who ran for the New Democrats at the end of the 1980s.

A Call from the Prime Minister's Office

A few days after the publication of Christine St-Pierre's letter, and for the first time since I had become managing director of News and Current Affairs, I received a call from Stephen Harper's office. Someone from the PMO wanted to inform me that the prime minister would be castigating Radio-Canada management for having suspended St-Pierre because of her positive statement about keeping Canadian troops in Afghanistan. Surprised by the call, I took care to specify that the prime minister should not use the expression "suspended"; in fact, I had reassigned the reporter to another beat because I considered that she had violated her obligation of neutrality as a parliamentary correspondent.

A few minutes later, in a scrum with the media, the prime minister did, in fact, criticize media outlets that would prevent journalists from expressing their support for the Canadian intervention in Afghanistan. Patriotism before journalism? That was not my style, but I was discovering it was that of the prime minister.

As these events were unfolding, I bumped into Rabinovitch and informed him of the call. A little smile flickered across his face, but he simply said, "I'm leaving you to manage this matter; I have faith in you."

This was the appropriate attitude for a president of CBC/Radio-Canada. Not panicking when politicians in power criticize decisions made by programming management and the News and Current Affairs Service. Respecting the arm's-length relationship between the government of the day and the public broadcaster. As head of News and Current Affairs, I was reassured to be able to rely on a president whose attitude reflected these principles. Otherwise, we risked opening the door to political interference, the temptation to coddle those in power, and, ultimately, the loss of all ability to think critically.

This would not be the only example of a collision between the PMO and News and Current Affairs management.

A Disturbing Inquiry

A year after Stephen Harper became prime minister, another issue flared up between the PMO and Radio-Canada's News and Current Affairs Service.

On January 27, 2007, we broadcast Guy Gendron's powerful documentary on the oil sands. Among other things, it unveiled the contents of a report by Natural Resources Canada that had been presented at an oil industry conference in Houston, Texas. The report clearly indicated that government policy was to plan for a quintupling of oil sands extraction. The report also recommended streamlining the environmental approvals process for energy projects.

The day after the broadcast, a shortened version of the documentary aired on the flagship 10:00 p.m. newscast, *Le Téléjournal*. Dimitri Soudas, then the prime minister's press secretary, emailed us, writing, "I am asking you to withdraw what SRC insinuated on last night's *Téléjournal*." He said that the meeting in Houston had been organized several weeks before the election of the Harper government, and therefore under Paul Martin's Liberal government, which was true. The report on the current affairs program *Zone libre enquêtes*, titled "Du sable dans l'engrenage" ("Sand in the Gears"), a preview of the complete version to be broadcast the following day, did not state the contrary. However, two different introduction scripts for the first broadcast on the radio newscast (*Le Radiojournal*) contained an error that associated the report solely with the Harper government. This required a correction, which we broadcast without hesitation.

However, we knew that Harper's new Conservative government attached great importance to the development of the oil sands.

Our report was very well documented. We had used Prime Minister Harper's speech to the Economic Club in New York as a source:

> The production from Alberta's oil sands — the second largest proven petroleum reserves on the planet — stands at more than a million barrels a day — on its way to four million a day by 2015. [10]

The speech was then repeated like a chorus by several of his ministers, including Natural Resources Minister Gary Lunn on January 17, 2007, in a press conference. Here is an excerpt:

> Oil sands, without question, many of you know, are the second largest oil find in the world. Canada is the second known largest oil reserve in the world. And, as we see potential increase in the production moving from a million barrels a day up to four or five, we need to do better. I think there is great promise in the oil sands for nuclear energy. Nuclear energy is emission free, there are no greenhouse gases and no pollutant is going up in this energy. Great opportunity.
>
> We've burned a lot of natural gas to extract that oil from the sands. There is great opportunity to pursue nuclear energy, something I'm very keen on. As far as the investments and the tax system, those are things that the minister of finance will have to look at. But I think we want to encourage companies to invest in technology that's going to have a dramatic reduction in greenhouse gases and have a strong benefit for the environment.

This was clearly government policy. Even if our documentary was indisputably in the public interest, the Prime Minister's Office did not see it the same way as we did. This was because he was not in control of the message about his energy policy. In addition, on January 23, in a rare move, the PMO's director of communications, Sandra Buckler, filed an official complaint with the office of Radio-Canada's ombudsman, Renaud Gilbert. At the same time, her office ordered all elected Conservatives to boycott interview requests by any Radio-Canada journalists across Canada for the next few days. Even the reporters in regional stations were punished. This was unheard of!

It was absolutely out of the question for us to renege on our responsibilities. We did our duty, as usual. We fact-checked the documentary again, as well as all subsequent reports, but without panicking and without the supervision or interference of anyone from senior management.

At the time, the war between Radio-Canada and the Quebecor Group was in full swing. Pierre Karl Péladeau was conducting a merciless battle against the public broadcaster. He had launched a lawsuit against the vice-president, Sylvain Lafrance, who had described Péladeau's decision to withdraw Quebecor from the Canadian Media Fund (which helps broadcasters and independent producers finance Canadian programming) as thuggish behaviour (Lafrance had used the word *voyou*). Péladeau was also lobbying the CRTC to refuse Radio-Canada's request to order the large cable and satellite distributors to increase their contribution to the fund. Finally, his media outlets took every possible opportunity to denigrate Radio-Canada's management and to publish a multitude of negative articles about the public broadcaster.

The Quebecor Group was also using Access to Information legislation to pepper the public broadcaster with requests for documents in the hope of finding examples of Radio-Canada wasting public funds.

On top of all that, Péladeau had ready access to the Prime Minister's Office. He had developed a good relationship with Kory Teneycke, Stephen Harper's director of communications from 2008 to 2010. Tenycke had facilitated a 2009 invitation for Julie Snyder and Pierre-Karl Péladeau to attend a private reception at Harper's residence, 24 Sussex Drive.

Given this context, it is not surprising that the conflict between Radio-Canada News and Current Affairs and the PMO's Sandra Buckler was followed by a smear campaign against the public broadcaster in the *Journal de Montréal.*

So it was that on January 25, 2007, Dany Bouchard wrote this vicious allegation: "Behind the scenes, people are whispering that the Radio-Canada report could be motivated by revenge against the Harper government, which has greenlit a process to reform the mandate and the financing of the public broadcaster."[11]

This was an odious and unfounded accusation. The team[12] that had produced the documentary filed an official complaint against *Le Journal de Montréal* and Dany Bouchard at the Quebec Press Council.

In the meantime, on February 1, we sent the PMO our official response to the Buckler complaint. Obviously we supported our report and the work of the *Zone libre enquêtes* team, while acknowledging one error, which was to have used the wrong date for the swearing-in of Minister Rona Ambrose. We had used February 6 instead of February 16. This certainly did not constitute a reason to question the entire program.

Nevertheless, the headline of the February 2, 2007, edition of the *Journal de Montréal*, on the first page of the Arts and Entertainment section — page 49 — told a very different story. Above a huge picture of Stephen Harper with a stranglehold around the Radio-Canada tower in Montreal was the headline: "Zone libre report on the oil sands. The public broadcaster acknowledges its share of errors. Read on page 55." Then, on page 55, "Zone libre: sand in the gearbox. The public broadcaster recognizes its mistakes." The article included three photos: one of Harper, one of Guy Gendron, and one of me.

It was an "anything goes" environment and a new kind of media war. The article included a misleading quote from an early draft of our response, not the version we had actually sent to the PMO. It seemed that a mole had provided the document to the *Journal de Montréal*.

From now on, we would have to be more careful.

The tone had been set. The war with the Quebecor empire, and particularly with *Le Journal de Montréal* and Sun Media, was clearly declared and underway.

On November 7, 2007, the Quebec Press Council handed down its decision in this matter. It upheld the complaint filed by the *Zone libre enquêtes* team against the *Journal de Montréal* and Dany Bouchard on three counts: false information, publication of unsubstantiated rumours, and failure of their responsibility to provide balanced information.

On the PMO front, we received no feedback to our response to Sandra Buckler, Stephen Harper's director of communications. There was no appeal to the ombudsman, and therefore no review on his part. However, the prime minister's press secretary, Dimitri Soudas,[13] began to examine everything we did, and he was not shy to let us know it. Volumes of emails to our management and our Ottawa bureau chiefs testify to his intense scrutiny.

Interventions from a Press Secretary

During the 2008 election campaign, Dimitri Soudas was not only the prime minister's press secretary — he was also his principal adviser for Quebec. Faithful to his habits, he wrote to us regularly. In an email on September 28, the month before the election, he attacked us for what we called fact-checking reports in our newscasts:

> ... many reports seem very critical with regard to the platform announced by the Conservative Party of Canada without being as critical towards the elements of response put forward by our political adversaries. Others seem relatively sympathetic to other parties rather than presenting the information in a factual manner. Here are a few reports that you could analyse (note that several are presented under the "fact-checking" banner): Cutbacks in culture (C. Kovacs) – September 12th, 2008, Relevance of the Bloc (F. Labbé) – September 15th, 2008, Daycare services (C. Kovacs) – September 17th, 2008, Young offenders (C. Kovacs) – September 26th, 2008.

A few days before the launch of the 2008 election campaign, he had insisted on being received in our Montreal offices. It does happen that during election campaigns we meet with representatives of the various political parties to learn more about their strategies and to plan the logistics of campaign coverage. Therefore, I had no objection to his meeting our people in charge of campaign coverage. However, I refused to participate in the meeting. I was under no obligation to do so. As managing director of News and Current Affairs, I wanted to keep the arm's-length relationship with the prime minister's representative, and it was out of the question for me to treat him as if he were more important than those from the other parties on the eve of an election. I learned subsequently that Soudas had been offended by my decision not to meet him. This set the tone for subsequent events.

We knew that the political parties paid close attention to the work of the journalists in Radio-Canada's News and Current Affairs Service. This explains why in every election campaign, I was in the habit of contracting with an independent and well-known organization, the Centre d'études sur les médias, to evaluate our election coverage as a whole. In 2008, the CEM's team of experienced experts came to the conclusion that Radio-Canada's News and Current Affairs Service had done a good job throughout the election campaign.

To be honest, we had to acknowledge that some on-air remarks by entertainment programming hosts outside News and Current Affairs may have left the impression that they were opposed to the Conservative Party. For example, some hosts of cultural programs did not hesitate to sign a petition opposing the Harper government's policies with regard to culture. Once again, these were not journalists working in News and Current Affairs, but I remain of the opinion that these people neglected their duty of reserve.

The Arrival of Hubert Lacroix

The tense relationship with the Conservative government presaged difficult times for Radio-Canada and its News and Current Affairs Service.

Appointed in 1999, Robert Rabinovitch finished his term as president in the fall of 2007.

There were all kinds of machinations to find his successor. The most optimistic among us hoped that the successful candidate would be a neutral personality who embodied the values of public service. Sylvain Lafrance, the vice-president of French Services, hoped for a time that he would be the chosen one.

I have been told that he was solicited as a candidate by an executive recruiter, who spoke to him about an interview in August 2007. Lafrance never had the promised interview. The process was short-circuited by a last-minute intervention. The day of the planned interview, the chair of the board, Tim Casgrain, told Lafrance that he would have to give up his presidential ambitions.

At the time, the Conservative government's strongman in Quebec was Senator Michael Fortier.[14] As it happens, he knew Hubert T. Lacroix very well. The two men were friendly enough that they socialized with their respective spouses. They also worked together on several boards; both were corporate lawyers. According to some sources, it was Fortier who recommended Lacroix for the presidency of the CBC. The appointment was announced by Minister of Canadian Heritage Josée Verner.

I learned an amusing anecdote about the background to this story. This was not the first time that Hubert Lacroix and Sylvain Lafrance had competed with one another. Back in 2005, Lacroix had applied for the position of vice-president of French Services at CBC/Radio-Canada under President Rabinovitch. The job had become available after the departure of Daniel Gourd.[15] At that time, Lafrance had won the day. This was probably the beginning of the tense relationship between the two men. In the covering letter to the Briefing Book that Robert Rabinovitch prepared for his successor, he insisted once again on one major point:

> CBC/Radio-Canada is a large and complex creative organization that can sometimes be frustrating, but always exciting. I am proud of having led this unique and critical institution and I am sure you will feel the same.
>
> There is one issue that is very dear to me, which I wish to bring to your attention. That is the arm's-length relationship with government, which is enshrined in the Broadcasting Act. It is critical to this country that the Corporation retains its editorial and journalistic independence from external forces in order to remain a true public broadcaster, and not a state broadcaster. This is the reason that the appointment of the President & CEO is not at pleasure[16] and that the Corporation reports to Parliament through the Minister of Heritage.[17] At times some try to shorten this relationship and we must defend it. It is not always easy, but it must be done if the public broadcaster is to survive.[18]

The outgoing president's concern would prove to be well founded.

CHAPTER 9

The Lacroix Style

Hubert T. Lacroix began his first mandate as president of CBC/Radio-Canada in January 2008. We began to discover he had a very different personality from that of his predecessor. Although he was rather cold and distant, he nevertheless insisted on being called by his first name. "Mr. Lacroix is my father; I'm Hubert," he repeated incessantly. He also insisted when speaking French on the use of the familiar *tu* rather than the formal *vous*. While some people saw this as a lack of pretension, others were truly uneasy practising this phony familiarity.

The new boss was an elite athlete who had excelled at basketball during his student days at Collège Brébeuf and then at McGill University. He had also been an elite basketball coach. This was, in fact, the way in which he had first become involved with Radio-Canada during the Summer Olympics of 1984, 1988, and 1996. He had even been hired as a colour commentator for basketball games on radio and television.

The man was also an excellent marathon runner, which was reflected in his generally ascetic appearance. He did not like overly simplified situations. As a marathon runner, he thought that things had to be achieved the hard way. In addition, even if he did know a little about the media, he knew absolutely nothing about television. As a lawyer he had specialized in mergers and acquisitions, and he had chaired the board of Télémédia from 2000 to 2005. The company owned private radio stations and general-interest magazines. He also lacked any particular insight into the workings of the federal government.

For the first while — quite a long time, actually — the staff at Radio-Canada found the new president charming. He showed concern over everyone's smallest problems and reached out directly by email to dozens of employees and middle managers. He managed the enterprise while occasionally intervening personally to settle a situation about which employees had been complaining for a long time. However, with regard to the senior managers at the top of the French networks, myself among them, he was suspicious. For example, we were told that he was convinced that members of French network management were charging their lunches to the corporation every day. He went as far as to investigate this several times, obviously finding nothing to substantiate his suspicions.

What was his vision of Radio-Canada as a public service broadcaster? At the time, Sylvain Lafrance was surprised at the first question Hubert Lacroix asked him when his appointment was announced on November 19, 2007: "Why the expression 'Radio-Canada, instrument of democracy and culture?' What do you mean? It's a company, a business ..."

On the occasion of my own first one-on-one encounter with the new president, in January 2008, I had also repeated this French services slogan, which was a good way of expressing my own philosophy of public broadcasting. He pursed his lips and said, "Oh yes, Sylvain is always talking to me about that ..."

From that point on, I understood that our respective visions were incompatible.

The new president didn't much like the management team around him. He did not like his vice-presidents to outshine him. The vice-president of French Services, Sylvain Lafrance, was already a leader who was appreciated, established, and known for his enlightened understanding of the future of the media. He had successfully led the organization to major rating increases on radio and great successes in television programming. In his own way, the vice-president of English Services, Richard Stursberg, also outstripped the president in the depth of his knowledge of the organization and the world of telecommunications, having been deputy minister of communications under Marcel Masse. In fact, the new president wondered why on earth he needed two vice-presidents. A few months after his appointment, he organized a lunch with both of them at a Montreal restaurant. There he told them, "At the end of the day, there are three of us doing the same job." No matter how much the vice-presidents tried to convince him of their usefulness and of the necessary allocation of responsibilities, Lacroix did not see things the same way. His vice-presidents also tried to define what they saw as the president's role. They explained that it was necessary to have someone with the mandate of representing CBC/Radio-Canada in Ottawa to deal with all the parties and senior bureaucrats in order to ensure that the role of public broadcaster was well understood. But Lacroix felt that his job was to manage day-to-day operations ... as if he had two vice-presidents too many.

One day, he organized an enormous conference, inviting only certain carefully selected employees. Only a handful of executives were invited. The objective was to have a direct dialogue with the artisans, those who did the real work, he said. The employees present were charmed, but the management people were offended, seeing in the whole exercise a confirmation of a lack of confidence in them. They were not wrong, as nearly all of the senior managers in French Services were replaced between 2008 and 2012.

In addition to all this, it would have been fair to expect that once he had been appointed, Lacroix would abandon his other activities to devote himself fully to the presidency of CBC/Radio-Canada,[1] an enormous task. But he did not see it that way.

It is important to emphasize that the president and CEO of CBC/Radio-Canada is one of the highest paid executives in any of the Canadian government's departments, agencies, and Crown corporations. My sources tell me that his salary was approximately $400,000 a year with an annual bonus of 10 percent. There are only three or four other mandarins in the public service ranked CEO7, and Lacroix is probably the highest paid of this group. The only more highly paid executive is the governor of the Bank of Canada, the sole federal employee in the CEO8 category.

The president of CBC/Radio-Canada also enjoys an additional perk that does not appear in the official documents about the presidency. Lacroix has a private chauffeur. The chauffeur is a resident of Ottawa, but he receives a travel allowance for his many trips, especially to Montreal, since the president works almost exclusively there.

No doubt, this salary is justified by the heavy obligations of the assignment. The challenges that any president and CEO of CBC/Radio-Canada must face are great; it is possible that in the context of the times, the new president was facing even greater challenges than those of his predecessors. In 2008, we were at the very epicentre of great changes in traditional media. The digital revolution was pulverizing media consumption habits and provoking a collapse of the traditional media. All media were competing fiercely on the same battleground. In 2008, it was also obvious that the public broadcaster was unpopular with the Conservative government and that its budget was once again threatened. Finally, media concentration in the country had reached a peak, and the various groups were waging war with one another. In Quebec, this resulted in the constant struggle between Radio-Canada and Quebecor.

In spite of all this, the new president had managed to negotiate permission in his contract to maintain his activities as a member of two external boards.

And yet the act considers this important position to be full time. Article 42 of the Broadcasting Act defines the role of the president and CEO as follows:

> Powers, duties and functions
> 42. (1) The President is the chief executive officer of the Corporation and has supervision over and direction of the work and staff of the Corporation and may exercise such powers and shall perform such other duties and functions as are assigned to the President by the by-laws of the Corporation.
>
> Full-time
> (2) The President shall perform the duties and functions of the office on a full-time basis.[2]

Other presidents had been given this type of authorization in the past. For example, Robert Rabinovitch was allowed to remain on the board of McGill University, a volunteer commitment. This was mentioned publicly on the occasion of his appointment in 1999.

For Hubert T. Lacroix, things were done differently. We learned only later about the nature of his other commitments. Nothing was said about them when he assumed the office.

Neither were they the same type of boards as Rabinovitch's McGill commitment. Unlike his predecessor, Lacroix was paid for his participation, until 2011 and 2012, on the boards of two companies that were very active in the financial markets.

The first, Fibrek, was in the forest products sector. He had been chair of its board since 2002. The second, Zarlink Semiconductor, specialized in telecommunications equipment. He remained a director and chaired its audit committee until 2011.

For his involvement with Fibrek, Lacroix was paid $85,250 in 2011, of which $25,250 was in attendance fees, $25,000 for his role as a director, and $35,000 in additional remuneration for his role as chair (president) of the board.[3]

A second presidency, therefore....

His commitment to Fibrek must certainly have kept him busy a few hours a week, especially during the time of a hostile takeover attempt by Produits forestiers Résolu (Abitibi Bowater). At the end of December 2011, this led Lacroix to wage a long judicial battle at every possible level[4] to repel the hostile takeover.

The struggle went on for several months.

Lacroix and the other board members were forced to resign in May 2012 after the shareholders finally accepted the offer from Produits forestiers Résolu.

> Management and board members of Fibrek had fought tooth and nail to prevent the takeover by Produits forestiers Résolu. It is therefore not surprising that Résolu replaced them all following its victory.[5]

An important detail: just before leaving Fibrek, the board and its chair did manage to vote themselves very advantageous severance payments.

The secretary-general of the board, Emmanuelle Lamarre-Cliche, also vice-president of legal affairs and sustainability, received at least $671,931[6] in severance pay.

A few months later, Lacroix put pressure on Louis Lalande, vice-president of French Services, to hire Emmanuelle Lamarre-Cliche. He accepted and appointed her his chief of staff in the fall of 2012.

With regard to the second business enterprise, Zarlink Semiconductor, where Hubert Lacroix was both a director and chair of the Audit Committee, a scenario similar to what had happened at Fibrek took place. It should be noted that in each fiscal quarter, Lacroix's duties to this board involved attending three consecutive days of meetings.

There again, the president of CBC/Radio-Canada was very busy; Zarlink Semiconductor was also the object of a hostile takeover offer. In this case, the offer was from an American entity, Microsemi Corporation. Once again, Lacroix was deeply involved with his fellow directors to fight the offer, but it was in vain. Nevertheless, the transaction brought him a big dividend.

Zarlink was purchased in September 2011 by the Microsemi Corporation. The notice circulated by the board on September 27, signed by Lacroix, says, "a director will receive a cash payment of $108,456 if the revised Microsemi offer is accepted." The management circular also informs us that Lacroix held 165,000 shares of Zarlink and that he had received $68,188 for his services as a director the year before.[7]

With such a volume of activity, we are well short of the full-time basis defined for the president and CEO of CBC/Radio-Canada in the Broadcasting Act, a duty for which he is well compensated.

The Conservative Party and Hubert T. Lacroix

Upon arriving in office, Lacroix benefited from a genuinely warm welcome inside the organization. There were no particular suspicions about him or his political links with the Conservative government. His affinities with the Conservative movement seemed to be limited to his good relations with the senator and minister Michael Fortier.

On October 14, 2008, Fortier lost the election in the riding of Vaudreuil-Soulanges. In the weeks to follow, the president pressured Sylvain Lafrance to ensure that French News and Current Affairs offer his friend and benefactor a contract. There were many remarks about this, notably from the vice-president. The more insistently the president pushed, the more I wanted to resist.

We did try to offer Fortier a kind of regular commentary on the all-news network RDI. He refused it. What he wanted was to be on the air as an "economic expert" and not to have to answer any questions about current political events. On our side, we insisted that he could not dissociate the two, especially since he had until recently been a cabinet minister in the Conservative government. This could not be ignored. We explained to him that we could certainly not ask our hosts to ask him questions only about economic matters. The talks ended there.

I was not unhappy with this outcome. I was not thrilled at the idea of having to welcome a friend of the president as a regular commentator. Of course, he was welcome to come on the air as an expert on specific issues.

The issue of the relationship between the president and the Conservative party also surfaced in November 2008 on the occasion of an event in Toronto that brought together about two hundred members of management from both the French and English Services. The event, which was baptized the Leaders' Forum, gave us insight into the new president's deeply held values.

Alone on stage, wearing jeans and an open-collared shirt, he paced back and forth, trying to galvanize his troops to confront future challenges. His words were measured and punctuated with frequent silences. The hour was perilous....

But he was only the star of the first part of the show. More was still to come. A surprise guest appeared on stage, a big, buff guy with the aura of a true leader having confronted real enemies. It was none other than General Rick Hillier, former chief of defence staff in the Canadian Armed Forces.[8] He was the one who had convinced Canadian authorities to place troops into combat zones in Afghanistan in 2003. For Lacroix, General Hillier embodied the leadership model to inspire the leaders inside his organization.

A deep uneasiness came over all of my colleagues from News and Current Affairs, both from Radio-Canada and from CBC. Remember that in 2008, Canada was still in full military deployment in Afghanistan. Many Canadians wanted the government to bring the troops home. Throughout the year, the government had announced that the Canadian Army's counter-insurrection operation in the province of Kandahar would continue until July 2011.

I had made the decision two years earlier to reassign Christine St-Pierre because she had taken an overt position in that controversial debate, ignoring her obligation to remain neutral.[9] CBC's Journalistic Standards and Practices defines the obligation of impartiality as follows:

> We provide professional judgment based on facts and expertise. We do not promote any particular point of view on matters of public debate.[10]

And here was the president of the public broadcaster convening us as cheerleaders in the company of his motivational speaker, General Hillier! To add insult to injury, the president had invested $25,000 of CBC/Radio-Canada's fast-disappearing resources (plus travel expenses and per diems) in General Hillier's one-hour appearance.

It demonstrated a flagrant lack of judgment. In such circumstances, Radio-Canada must obviously keep its distance and not take positions on "matters of public debate."

Fortunately for him, no media reported on either the event or the surprise guest. If this had happened, the impartiality of both CBC and Radio-Canada, especially their English and French News and Current Affairs, would have been compromised. There was at the very least an appearance of conflict of interest. I am certain that he never understood the extent to which he had placed the entire organization in a vulnerable situation. Lacroix seemed concerned only with expressing open admiration for his star keynote speaker.

We suddenly understood that we were now fully in the world of Stephen Harper's Conservatives, of which military culture is a notoriously open part.

If it is true that the relationship between the Liberals and Radio-Canada had been particularly difficult in the 1970s, we were feeling that the next decade would bring more of the same. The presence of Conservative political power was increasingly felt in the public service. We all understood that we would have to be on guard if we wanted to protect the organization's impartiality.

The Fox in the Henhouse

As we have seen, the law defines an independent status for Radio-Canada. However, it can be very difficult to protect this status when the board is made up of directors chosen more for their political allegiance than for their competence.

We are forced to acknowledge that the selection of board members happens today according to unpublished criteria that appear to be driven by partisan political considerations. The directors are chosen by the prime minister or the minister of Canadian heritage, and the appointments are submitted to neither Parliament nor the Standing Committee on Canadian Heritage.

Whatever the party in power, this appointment process is entirely inappropriate for a service that needs to operate independently in order to do its job properly. In fact, the Caplan-Sauvageau report had included reforming the appointment process among its recommendations.

Of course I have had many opportunities to interact with competent board members who clearly understood both their role and the arm's-length principle. Some of them are still on the board, but they are rare. The current members of the board are all partisan Conservatives, and several have contributed money to the Conservative Party, as is shown in a chart published by Friends of Canadian Broadcasting on April 30, 2013.[11]

Rémi Racine, who has sat on the board since 2008 and has chaired it since 2012, is a good example. His qualifications and expertise are premised on his role as CEO of Behaviour Interactive (formerly A2M), a video game business that must keep him busy, since it has nearly three hundred employees in Montreal and in Santiago, Chile.

The main reason for his appointment is no doubt his close links to the Conservative Party. One thing is certain: Radio-Canada did not seem to interest him very much. Some people have overheard him saying that he accepted the appointment only to serve the party.

He also told a member of my team in 2011 that he never listened to Radio-Canada's French radio service. He preferred Paul Arcand's morning show on the private 98.5 FM in Montreal.

Here is the way Rémi Racine described his Conservative Party affiliations to a reporter from *La Presse* in 2008, including the fact that he was national secretary of the party from 1989 to 1991:

> "The youngest ever," he said, emphasizing that he had participated in four election campaigns and that Ministers John Baird and Jim Prentice were members of his close circle of friends. Still a member of the Party, he does not hesitate to show his colours. "For me," he says, "politics is entertainment. It's fun, it's social. It's like playing golf." [12]

At the time of the article's publication, Racine had just been appointed to the board of directors of Radio-Canada. He also said this:

> When you get involved in a political party, it's because you care about society's problems. Afterwards, it is natural to end up in business associations, all kinds of things. [13]

Since assuming office, the chair of the board has had a major influence on certain important decisions at Radio-Canada.

For example, in 2012 he approached his cabinet connections to help obtain a presidential mandate renewal for Hubert Lacroix. My sources tell me that the president also supported Racine's candidacy as chair of the board. The situation is a somewhat unusual, since it is traditional to have an anglophone chair when the president is a francophone, and vice versa.

Another example of partisan appointments to the board is the 2011 arrival of Pierre Gingras, the mayor of Blainville from 1993 to 2005. In

May 2013, when he testified at the Charbonneau Commission inquiry into corruption in the construction industry, a certain Gilles Cloutier said he had donated $30,000 to Gingras's election campaign. At the time, Cloutier was an exceptional political organizer — a rainmaker — in municipal elections in the region of the lower Laurentians north of Montreal. His testimony showed that Gingras had benefited enormously from this. Here is an excerpt from a May 2, 2013, article in *Le Devoir* by Brian Myles, following Cloutier's testimony at the Charbonneau Commission:

> In 1997, Michel Déziel, who was still a lawyer at the time, was said to have talked to him [Gilles Cloutier] to help him "launder" $30,000 from [the construction company] Dessau…. According to Gilles Cloutier's testimony, the money was designated for Blainville's Action civique, the party of Mayor Pierre Gingras, who would become an ADQ Member of the National Assembly in 2007 and 2008.
>
> Mr. Gingras is today a member of the Board of Radio-Canada…. "He [Michel Déziel] committed a fraud. I wanted to mention it now that he is a judge," Mr. Cloutier told the Charbonneau Commission on Thursday.[14]

Cloutier's testimony prompted the Canadian Judicial Council to investigate Judge Déziel's past.

Another person mentioned Pierre Gingras's name at the Charbonneau Commission a few days later. He was retired engineer Roger Desbois. Here is how reporter Pierre-André Normandin, of *La Presse*, reported his remarks on May 22, 2013:

> In Blainville for example, Tecsult decided to support Daniel Ratthé as a candidate for the Mayoralty of Blainville in the 2005 election in order to maintain its market share in the Lower Laurentian municipality. Roger Desbois says he delivered $30,000 to the residence

of the former Mayor, Pierre Gingras, for the campaign
of his chosen successor.

Daniel Ratthé ultimately failed to be elected mayor.[15]

In the days after this story was published, Minister James Moore, responsible for CBC/Radio-Canada, announced that he would investigate the allegations against Pierre Gingras.[16] At the time of writing, Gingras was still on the CBC board.

In 2007, Gingras was elected to the National Assembly as a member of the Action démocratique du Québec (ADQ) caucus, led by Mario Dumont. At the time, the ADQ's chair of fundraising was Leo Housakos, who would later become the Conservative Party's lead fundraiser in Quebec. Defeated in the 2008 election, Gingras subsequently worked on the Conservative campaign. With Housakos, he organized a Conservative rally in Saint-Eustache to support Claude Carignan, the Conservative candidate in the riding of Deux-Montagnes. Carignan was not elected, but Stephen Harper subsequently appointed him to the Senate.

In 2009, Gingras headed up a financing campaign for Gilles Taillon, who wanted to succeed Mario Dumont as leader of the ADQ. Gingras became the intermediary between Taillon and the new Conservative fundraiser, Leo Housakos. In the light of all this, it is not surprising to see Taillon's change of heart towards the Conservatives' actions in Quebec, as described in this 2009 article from *Le Soleil*:

> The candidate Gilles Taillon changed his tune yesterday about the "Conservative takeover of the ADQ" which he had said he feared on Sunday, and on the interference of several Conservatives in the race. The man in charge of Taillon's financing organization, Pierre Gingras, nevertheless dined with an important Conservative fundraiser, Senator Leo Housakos, last Friday. [17]

It was the beginning of the political conversion of Pierre Gingras to the Conservative Party. Regardless of his past as a Liberal candidate in 2004, his rapprochement with Conservative Leo Housakos would serve him well. His services to the Conservative Party would suffice for Stephen Harper to appoint him in February 2011 to the CBC board for a mandate of five years. Nowhere on his resume is there evidence of any competence relevant to the world of communications, never mind the public broadcaster. He therefore represents the world of the Conservatives, not the world of the media.

Rémi Racine and Pierre Gingras are the Conservative government's two Quebec francophone representatives on the board of Radio-Canada, which is made up of twelve members, including the president.

Among the anglophone members of the board, the Conservative Party links are not limited to financial contributions. For example, George T.H. Cooper, briefly a Progressive Conservative MP in the Joe Clark minority government of 1979 (subsequently defeated in the 1980 election), has been on the board since May 9, 2008. He was first appointed for a four-year mandate, which was subsequently renewed for two years. In May 2015, Rob Jeffery was appointed to the board. Just three months earlier, he had finished a second term as treasurer of the Nova Scotia Progressive Conservative Party.

A Direct Line to the Government?

Hubert Lacroix knows how to pick his entourage. However, it is far from certain that he clearly understands the notion of keeping arm's length from political power. So it happened that on December 23, 2010, in the context of a federal government exchange program called Exchanges Canada, a certain Alfred McLeod was "loaned" to CBC for two years as director of corporate affairs. McLeod had come directly from the Privy Council Office, where his title was Assistant Deputy Minister, Intergovernmental Policy and Planning.

What is the Privy Council Office? The government's website defines its role as follows:

> The Privy Council Office (PCO) is the hub of nonpartisan, public service support to the Prime Minister and Cabinet and its decision-making structures. Led by the

Clerk of the Privy Council, PCO helps the Government implement its vision and respond effectively and quickly to issues facing the government and the country. [18]

What was McLeod coming to do at CBC/Radio-Canada? Implementing the vision of the government and the prime minister? Why did no one express the slightest discomfort at the idea of borrowing a senior public servant from the Privy Council Office?

In an exchange with Pierre Trudel, a lawyer who has often advised Radio-Canada's senior management on the notion of arm's length, he told me, "arm's length is like a muscle: if you don't exercise it, the muscle atrophies."[19] It was obvious that the muscle was getting flabby.

Alfred McLeod entered CBC/Radio-Canada discreetly — too discreetly, in fact. Very few people knew who he was and where he had come from. This is how a memo to senior management explained the reasons and the term of his presence in the organization: "... for a term of two years as part of the temporary executive exchange program known as 'Exchanges Canada' which offers senior executives an opportunity for personal and professional development, while stimulating knowledge transfer between different sectors...."[20]

This is how Alfred McLeod described himself in 2011 in an interview during a meeting in Australia:

> Since returning to Canada, I have started a new job. I am on a two-year assignment from the Government of Canada to the Canadian Broadcasting Corporation (CBC, which is our version of your ABC). I am Executive Director, Corporate Affairs and the focus of my work is the corporation's relationship with the federal government and its departments and agencies. What a difference from what I was doing before — every day still brings many opportunities to scratch my head and ask, "What the heck am I doing here?" It's great![21]

Yes, indeed, what the heck was he doing there?

McLeod participated in strategic discussions on the future of CBC/ Radio-Canada for two and a half years. When he left the organization in 2013, this is how his contribution was recognized:

> Alfred's achievements as Executive Director, Corporate Affairs at CBC/Radio-Canada over the past two and a half years have had a significant and positive impact on the Corporation. With his vast knowledge of the workings of the public service, he helped us move important initiatives along smoothly through the system and at the same time helped us engage senior leaders in the public service to build stronger working relationships.[22]

It is noteworthy that the person issuing this staff memo, Bill Chambers, had, among other positions, been chief of staff to Joe Clark when he was minister of foreign affairs in the Progressive Conservative government of Brian Mulroney, before joining CBC/Radio-Canada as vice-president of communications from 2003 to 2008. He is also the son of Egan Chambers, a former minister in the Diefenbaker government. After the arrival of Hubert Lacroix, Bill Chambers was promoted to vice-president of branding, communications, and corporate affairs. He had a major influence on the corporation's strategy until his resignation in August 2015. The loan of Alfred McLeod from the Privy Council Office had been his idea.

The recourse to the Exchanges Canada program was not over. Both sides had taken a liking to it.

On January 31, 2014, Chambers published a new memo:

> I have the pleasure of announcing the appointment of Marc O'Sullivan to the position of Director-General of Corporate Affairs. He succeeds Alfred MacLeod, whose term ended in the spring of 2013.[23]

Marc O'Sullivan came from the Treasury Board, where they know how to count. In the Treasury Board organizational chart, he was identified as assistant comptroller general, assets and acquired services, which is defined as follows:

> The Assets and Acquired Services Sector (ASAS) plays a lead role in supporting the commitment of the Office of the Comptroller General (OCG) to strengthening the management of assets and acquired services within the Government of Canada. [24]

In the memo announcing O'Sullivan's arrival, Chambers concluded,

> Without a doubt, Marc's expertise is timely for the Corporation. Join me in wishing him a stimulating and fruitful term at CBC/Radio-Canada. [25]

Armed with this expertise, O'Sullivan's arrival was timely in contributing to the discussions that would lead to the budget cuts of April 2014, which foreshadowed the elimination of 657 jobs over two years.[26]

The senior Treasury Board bureaucrat was there for the creation of the strategic plan titled *A Space for us All*,[27] CBC/Radio-Canada's 2015–2020 plan for its future.

These two loans of senior federal public servants were a first. It is hard not to think that these people, who would be returning to their old jobs after their time at CBC, would have a dual allegiance, and even that their primary allegiance would necessarily be to their principal employer, the government. The federal power has therefore had a mole at the highest levels of the public broadcaster since December 2010.

Another new arrival in the circle around Lacroix was Jodi White. A former CBC reporter, White is without a doubt a competent person with an impressive resumé. She has led businesses and organizations such as the Public Policy Forum of Canada, whose board she chaired. She chaired a special committee to redefine the role of the ombudsman at both Radio-Canada and CBC, tabled in 2012.

Jodi White has also played an important role in the history of the Progressive Conservative Party. In the 1997 election, under the leadership of Jean Charest, she chaired the Progressive Conservative campaign. She had also been chief of staff to the PC minister of foreign affairs, Joe Clark, in 1984 and 1988, as well as to Prime Minister Kim Campbell for a few months in 1993. Bill Chambers had succeeded her on Joe Clark's staff.

She also bestowed her friendship upon Hubert Lacroix. In the summer of 2010, he was seen at her cottage in North Hatley, Quebec, along with Jean Charest and their respective spouses. The president of CBC/Radio-Canada has rented a cottage in the same village for many years. The problem here is not a gathering of friends, but that it may have been a little unwise for the president of Radio-Canada to engage in private meetings with the leader of the Liberal Party and premier of Quebec. Let's remember the context. In an interview broadcast several months beforehand, on April 13, 2010, the former Quebec minister of justice, Marc Bellemare, had unburdened himself to Alain Gravel[28] to denounce the undue influence of Quebec Liberal Party fundraisers in matters such as judicial appointments. He added that the premier, Jean Charest, was fully aware of the problem. The team from the investigative program *Enquête* had been producing numerous reports on corruption in the construction industry and the illegal financing of political parties. The population was demanding a public inquiry, which Charest was resisting, despite the growing pressure.

In hindsight, many people are convinced that without the series of reports on this particular program, there would not have been a Charbonneau Commission in Quebec. The announcement of its creation, despite Jean Charest's misgivings, was made on October 19, 2011.

The president of CBC/Radio-Canada would have been wise, in the turbulent political environment of the summer of 2010 in Quebec, and because of the major role that his own organization's investigative journalists were playing in it, to show a little more reserve. Under the circumstances, it was clearly inappropriate to participate in these private encounters with the premier of Quebec.

Enquête and the President's Vision

The preceding year, during the 2009–2010 television season, I had bumped into the host of *Enquête*, Alain Gravel. He reported to me that he was worried about a strange conversation he had just had with the president in the elevator. Gravel had been proud to tell him, "Boss, we have a hell of a good show on *Enquête* tonight!" Lacroix replied, apparently perfectly seriously, "When are you going to have positive investigations?"

Gravel and I both came away with the impression that he did not find the purpose of our investigations relevant. We did laugh about it in the following days, but we knew from then on that our president was not one of the thousands of fans of our journalistic investigations, the ones that had so influenced the course of events in 2009, 2010, and 2011, and that had led to the creation of the Charbonneau Commission.

It seemed that he did not care whether or not we won many journalism awards for high-profile "shock" documentaries such as "Collusion frontale" ("Frontal Collusion"). In this documentary by Marie-Maude Denis and Alain Gravel, *Enquête* had lifted the veil on the existence of a select club of businesses that conspired to fix which among them would be the low bidder on RFPs for highway infrastructure. The group was made up of construction and engineering firms.

Everywhere, public organizations and media were praising Radio-Canada's News and Current Affairs Service for its contribution to cleaning up Quebec politics — everywhere but in the president's office, on the twelfth floor of Maison Radio-Canada in Montreal.

Good Relations with the Minister

In all the meetings I attended with Hubert Lacroix, he boasted of enjoying good relations with the minister of Canadian heritage, James Moore.[29] He was happy about this and seemed to have not the slightest reservation about the necessary critical distance of the CEO of the public broadcaster from the government of the day.

This is the same minister who intervened to force one of Radio-Canada's websites, Tou.tv, to take down the French series *Hard*, which he found offensive.

The controversy around the French production arose after a reporter from Sun Media attacked James Moore over a fictional series containing explicit sexual scenes. The minister said he never wanted to see that kind of offensive programming again.[30]

The preceding summer, on June 29, 2011, it was Moore who had emailed[31] the president of CBC/Radio-Canada during Prince William and Kate Middleton's cross-Canada visit. He wanted to make sure that both French and English News and Current Affairs Services would use the correct titles for Prince William and his spouse: the Duke and Duchess of Cambridge.

Lacroix hastened to forward the minister's email directly to the two senior executives in charge of News and Current Affairs, demanding a response:

> Hello Hubert,
> I was watching the CBC coverage this morning from the airport, while waiting for my flight to Ottawa. It's not a big problem, but I noticed it, so I thought I would mention this:
>
>> For protocol, Kate and William's visit is a "royal tour" not a "royal visit" as CBC has been saying on the air. They are not "visitors" to Canada, they are members of the Royal family and he is the future King of Canada. He is not visiting Canada. Furthermore, they are the Duke and Duchess of Cambridge, not "Will and Kate."

We were indeed in Stephen Harper's Conservative universe, in which royalty truly matters.

CHAPTER 10

The Conservative Style

It was obvious that James Moore appreciated the close collaboration that had been instituted between his government and CBC/Radio-Canada. On May 29, 2012, when he was still minister of Canadian heritage, he said:

> That's what we did with the CBC. We didn't work against them; we worked with them in this process, so that they have the funds available to deliver their 2015 plan. It's not going to be easy. They're going to have some challenges, there's no question, but they're going to be able to do it. A great deal of credit certainly goes to Hubert Lacroix, the president and CEO, the board, the management, and the team that they have there, who have I think come together with a really ambitious plan for the coming five years that will serve the country very well.[1]

Moore's support for Hubert Lacroix became obvious some time before he was renewed for a second mandate. It should be said that Lacroix was indeed delivering the goods. He was implementing the desired budget cuts efficiently and had downsized the corporation. He was accumulating bonus points.

A Philosophical Change

In the summer of 2012, the former national secretary of the Conservative Party, Rémi Racine, became chair of the board of CBC/Radio-Canada. He and Lacroix were good partners. Their strategy to guarantee the long-term survival of the organization was to push for greater commercialization of the public service.

In the 2010–2015 strategic plan, *Everyone, Every Way*,[2] we had seen a major philosophical change in direction: the discourse about an open window on the world, which had guided previous plans, was suddenly removed from the corporation's priorities. And yet it was a vital objective in an era of globalization. A few years later, in April 2013, management announced the cancellation of the international show *Une heure sur terre* (*An Hour on Earth*).[3] This was a strange decision at a time when francophone culture needs contact with the whole francophone universe to survive, when our business people need to understand the world to invest in it, and when we have to decide whether or not to participate in major global conflicts. Only a public broadcaster really has the means to offer international information with a Canadian point of view, especially on television, given its higher cost structure. We saw at the time of the Iraq war, for example, how different the Canadian point of view could be from that of the Americans. For the private broadcasters, this kind of coverage is too expensive and unprofitable.

In addition, we were talking more than ever about the importance of service to the regions. This shift appeared to contradict the budget cuts being imposed on other sectors. At this time, the CRTC had just created a special dedicated fund for local programming,[4] which allowed us to appear deceptively generous. Thanks to this funding, service to the regions was greatly improved. We could offer much more complete programming in important centres such as Sherbrooke, Trois-Rivières, and Rimouski on the French side, and Windsor and others on the English side. Supper-hour news shows were lengthened from half an hour to an hour on several stations. We were able to add regional time slots on our musical radio service, Espace Musique (now ICI Musique). In 2011, we created several new web journalism jobs to cover the regions north and south of Montreal. By 2014, there were only two reporters left, and the premises we had rented in Laval and Brossard were almost unused. The national programs also undertook many coast-to-coast tours at great expense.

Unfortunately, the times of abundance were short-lived. The CRTC eliminated the temporary funding completely by September 2014, and all local news enrichment that had been made possible under the program had to be cut once the funding disappeared. While regional services are still part of CBC/Radio-Canada's fundamental values, they have to be cut now too.

This is a good example of how difficult it is to plan and to manage an institution such as CBC/Radio-Canada in the absence of stable long-term funding.

For some, this regional orientation, especially when it was code for reaching francophone minorities outside Quebec, was a new way to promote and build the Canadian nation. The increased airtime for other provinces prompted online comments asserting that Radio-Canada was thereby inciting Quebec francophones to return to the days when they defined themselves as French Canadians.

In fact, the objective of bringing together francophones (and all Canadians) from coast to coast dates back to the creation of the CBC, and the federal government has never abandoned the idea. Every time CBC/Radio-Canada management appears in front of a federal body, there are questions from MPs, senators, or CRTC commissioners focusing on the subject of the on-air coverage of other provinces besides Quebec. In the excerpt below from a February 27, 2014, article in *L'Acadie nouvelle*, Hubert Lacroix clearly expresses his ideas on the subject for the benefit of the paper's Acadian readership:

> The first thing we did was to recruit two new full-time correspondents for the nightly *Téléjournal*: one in Edmonton and one in Moncton. Instantly, there was a share of mind and a follow-up on news items to feed the *Téléjournal*.... The *Téléjournal* is changing. I hope that you can see it. You will notice it and you could conclude with us that the

measures we have put in place in the regions, the regional panels, our increasing efforts to gather this information and to reflect it on the air, on radio and on television, I hope that you will see our efforts.[5]

Obviously, this raises the never-ending issue of the relative share of airtime between Quebec and the other provinces in Radio-Canada's programming. The institution has always been torn between two opposing imperatives: on the one hand, the needs of francophones in Quebec, who make up more than 90 percent of the French-language audience and whose fidelity brings in substantial commercial revenues, and on the other, the truly legitimate needs of French-speaking citizens in the other provinces, who are scattered in small numbers across the country and whose issues, it has to be said, often cause the Quebec audience to tune out.

It is an ongoing challenge for Radio-Canada to find the right balance to meet everyone's needs. Whether we like it or not, it would be surprising if this problem resolved itself just because a government or a president decides to bolt an artificially contrived vision onto the institution.

An Awkward Omission

Here is an anecdote that speaks volumes about the way the current president sees the newsgathering process: in February 2014, while he was visiting CBC/Radio-Canada's Washington bureau, Hubert Lacroix mentioned to a few employees, including French network correspondent Joyce Napier and the English network's Neil Macdonald, that some Conservatives were complaining that both networks were talking too much about the Senate spending scandal.

The reporters were uneasy. The spending scandal around senators Mike Duffy, Pamela Wallin, and Patrick Brazeau was in full swing. It was entirely normal that the newscasts would be covering it. The reporters present told their CBC colleagues and their bosses what they had heard from the president.

It was also in February 2014 that we learned that Lacroix had been forced to reimburse the public purse for $30,000 in living expenses that he had claimed for his stays in the nation's capital. The president of CBC/Radio-Canada was appearing before a Senate committee, and Conservative Senator Don Plett took advantage of the opportunity to grill him on the subject: "Do you not think, sir, that the public would be just as outraged about your misappropriating expenses as anyone else?"[6] the senator asked the president.

At the same time, the senator expressed his anger about the many reports on CBC and Radio-Canada about the allegedly fraudulent conduct of his colleagues from the upper chamber.

Lacroix pleaded guilty to having made an error in good faith while claiming duplicate living expenses. "I am angry at myself for not having clarified the rules surrounding my expenses when I was first appointed," said Lacroix. "… I want to apologize to all those Canadians who support CBC/Radio-Canada for this careless error."[7]

In fact, Lacroix was already receiving a monthly allowance of $1,500, which was to cover his expenses when he travelled to Ottawa. He was not entitled to claim additional expenses. It may well be true that the board had not established very clear rules. But we can still ask ourselves how it was that the president had not noticed that he was double dipping over a period of five years for the same expenses. And, of course, no congratulations are due to the internal auditors for speed and competence.

"Duceppe? …" Writes James Moore

Under the guise of maintaining good relations with Minister James Moore, the president showed excessive zeal. On August 18, 2011, as I did every year, I attended the seasonal program launch on Radio-Canada's Première Chaîne (the French-language equivalent of Radio One on CBC). What struck me that day was a comment on Twitter about Gilles Duceppe, who had been defeated in the May 2 election a few months previously. We were announcing that he would be one of a team of commentators on the program *Médium large*, hosted by Catherine Perrin. Even senior management of French Radio was not aware of this catch. I was a little surprised, but not nearly as much as the president. The former leader of the Bloc Québécois, a regular on our airwaves? All hell broke loose on the twelfth floor! Lacroix was running around with a cryptic email from Moore in his hands:

Duceppe? … James Moore.

The president was beside himself. Encountering Patrick Beauduin, then managing director of French Radio,[8] he conveyed his surprise both at the news and the minister's email.

The president pressured Beauduin to change course and, at the very least, avoid having Duceppe talking politics on Radio-Canada's airwaves. Within just a few minutes, Lacroix had made multiple interventions among members of senior management of French Services.

In the meantime, Anne Sérode, who was director of Première Chaîne radio,[9] had no idea what was going on one floor above her. She did, however, want to clarify the terms of the surprise agreement that had been made between the members of her team and the outgoing leader of the Bloc Québécois.

Although she was a bit worried, she had asked Duceppe to come and meet her at Radio-Canada to discuss the subject matter on which he would be commenting in his appearances on *Médium large*. A respectful conversation took place in Sérode's office. Duceppe was very happy to participate in the program. He thought everything had been settled, but he would soon find out that this was not the case. In order to better define his role on the show, there was a format change on the table. In the course of the discussion, he understood clearly that he was being kept clear of political subjects. After two phone calls, he made his decision: it was no. The final proposal was not consistent with the oral agreement he had reached a few days earlier with the producer *of Médium large*, Bernard Michaud, and the host, Catherine Perrin. The director of la Première Chaîne and Duceppe agreed to announce his withdrawal in a joint release:

Montréal, Wednesday, August 17th, 2011 — Following a misunderstanding on the nature of his mandate, Gilles

Duceppe has chosen not to become a weekly commentator on the program *Médium large*.[10]

Afterwards, I met with Duceppe. He told me that he was offended,
because there had been no misunderstanding on his side. It was Radio-
Canada that had completely reversed itself on the terms of the original
agreement!

The director of la Première Chaîne swore that she had not heard
about political interference or pressure from the president at the time of
her meeting with Duceppe.

If she had, she says, "I would have had a problem doing things." It was
therefore only after the meeting with Duceppe that Beauduin informed
her about the discussions that had been going on and the pressure from
on high. He had sought to protect his colleague.

Sérode adds, "I never had a mandate to get Duceppe off our airwave,
because I had no idea what had happened on the twelfth floor."[11]

As for me, there had been an attempt to get me to attend the
meeting to "clarify Radio-Canada's journalistic policies" for Duceppe.
I had categorically refused. I had no business there. I was already aware
of James Moore's email, and it was therefore out of the question. I did
not want to be drawn into this operation as an accomplice; I wanted
to maintain my independence and my integrity. This was a flagrant
example of the absence of the arm's-length relationship between Radio-
Canada and the government of the day. Moore had no business dictating
programming choices, particularly as it is entirely normal for Radio-
Canada to present commentators of all political stripes, and no one
had established that Gilles Duceppe's presence on *Médium large* would
disturb the balance of opinions being presented.

A month later, in September, the president came to chair the French
Services management meeting in person. For my colleagues and me,
it was our first meeting without Sylvain Lafrance, who would officially
leave his position the next month. In the course of this meeting, the president told us that he would be naming an interim replacement at the top
of French Services. He also took advantage of the opportunity to talk at
length about the Duceppe matter.

Patrick Beauduin remembers the moment well: "Hubert had said something like, 'What lack of judgment, to hire Duceppe for a radio program!'"[12]

For my part, I was sitting across from Beauduin. I remember watching my colleague flinch, flabbergasted at being so severely taken to task in front of his colleagues.

The former head of French Radio also remembers an important detail:

> When Hubert talks to us, he always makes an explicit link between the discussions he is having about the next budget and risk that "our" decisions are causing for future public funding. A clear allusion to the fact that we need to be more "understanding" or show more "discretion"...[13]

I can testify that the president also lit into me at the same meeting, telling me that there was too much anti-Conservative talk on the air: "I've raised this with you before, Alain..."

Anne Sérode, director of la Première Chaîne, also remembers another Lacroix intervention in the same vein, this one in April 2012:

> This was strictly a management meeting. No employees. And it was all platforms, television/radio/web. Hubert said, "We are not the only ones affected by budget cuts; many ministries will also have reduced means. We will therefore behave like good 'corporate' citizens, we will not oppose these cuts, and I am counting on you to make sure that the airwaves are not used for self-pity."[14]

I want to be clear here. I believe that members of CBC/Radio-Canada management are perfectly entitled to evaluate what they hear on the air and to adjust the direction if it becomes necessary because of a violation of the organization's journalistic standards or program policies. But that said, a CEO who demonstrates such abject collusion with the politicians in power loses that right, in my eyes, because he has amply proven that his judgment is rooted in political criteria that have nothing to do with the rules of journalism.

While government representatives threatened to cut off our funding whenever they didn't like what they heard on the airwaves, it is important to speak up loudly and to denounce this odious political blackmail. I can understand that Lacroix felt cornered by this, but he should have known that the more you give in to this kind of tactic, the more you encourage its use.

A Housecleaning in Senior Management

Hubert Lacroix had another idea in the back of his mind. Late in 2012, he was in the middle of a charm offensive to convince the government to renew his mandate as president — a plan he had been preparing for some time. He needed to demonstrate that he had the place well in hand, that he was the man of the hour for the Stephen Harper government.

First step, then: get rid of certain obstacles, especially his most important senior executives.

If we go back in time, the first to go was Richard Stursberg, vice-president of English Services, who was fired on August 6, 2010. Lacroix commented on the departure of his second-in-command on the CBC side:

> We are in the midst of developing a new strategic plan that will guide CBC/Radio-Canada through the next five years. This is the opportune time to bring new leadership to English services and to ensure alignment of the senior team on the future of the public broadcaster.[15]

The president appointed Kirstine Stewart, but after three years the new leadership was not sufficiently "aligned" for the president's taste. Lacroix had been searching for a reason to get rid of his new vice-president of English Services. He discovered that Stewart's partner (now her husband) had worked openly for Justin Trudeau's Liberals and that he had even arranged a meeting at their family residence, ignoring his wife's duty of reserve from political activity. I can understand that this lapse of judgment would have quite rightly irritated the president. Not long after this incident, Stewart resigned to become head of Twitter Canada.

Once the housecleaning was done in English Services, Lacroix attacked French Services. It was Sylvain Lafrance's turn to be in the president's crosshairs. But how to get rid of a vice-president whose successes had brought so much public recognition?

Throughout 2010 and 2011, the president constantly stalked the vice-president, criticizing him at every turn. This was sometimes ludicrously petty. For example, when the French network's long-time and highly regarded news anchor, Bernard Derome, retired after many years of being the face of Radio-Canada's News Service, Lafrance thought it would be appropriate to give him some recognition and to thank him for his service by inviting him to lunch. After all, it was an exceptional event. The vice-president also wanted to offer Derome a role as ambassador of Radio-Canada's seventy-fifth anniversary celebrations. Although the bill was modest, Lacroix refused to pay for the lunch, calling it an unjustified expense.

This is only a small anecdote, but it gives an idea of the climate between the two men at the time.

Sylvain Lafrance negotiated his departure from Radio-Canada and left his office for the last time on Friday, October 21, 2011.

Dear Alain, It's Your Turn

Three days later, a well-informed person told me, "After Sylvain, you should know that you are the next one to be pushed out." I was a little surprised, although there had been doubt growing in my mind about whether my days as head of News and Current Affairs were numbered.

I had even begun making short notes in a personal diary similar to the one Raymond David had kept thirty years earlier.[16]

My diary starts on May 3, 2011, the day after the federal election:

> May 3rd — Federal election. Everybody is commenting about the news: the orange wave that swept away the Bloc. The real news is that for the first time in the

history of this country, a political party has been able to obtain a majority without Quebec!

After I realized that my future was at stake, an occasion soon arose that allowed me to test the waters.

It was June 22, 2011, a few weeks after the election of the majority Conservative government. I had been asked to make a presentation to the CBC board in conjunction with the vice-president of French Services, Sylvain Lafrance, who was to announce his intention of leaving his position that autumn to the board on that day. Our presentation was titled *The Diversity of Voices in our News and Current Affairs: Challenges, Perceptions and Accomplishments.*

Let's remember that all the members of this board of directors — all, without exception, according to my sources — are active partisans of the Conservative Party. In presenting to them, we made clear the importance that we attached to reflecting a diversity of voices in our programming. We also presented the findings of a study by the Centre d'études sur les médias, an independent organization mandated to analyze the French network's electoral coverage. Here is an excerpt from the centre's interim report:

> The broad conformity of our results from one media to another, and from one program to another, demonstrates that there is likely no bias in the Radio-Canada teams' attention to the different parties in the running.[17]

So, according to our experts, there had been no biases in Radio-Canada's coverage.

The aftermath is in my personal diary:

> June 22nd — Presentation to the board in Ottawa on equity and balance. Was "skinned alive" by P. Gingras about biased coverage of Harper and by R. Racine on the election night coverage. A tough moment. On my return, I say to my spouse: "It doesn't smell good ..."

"Skinned alive" is the right description. The charge came from former mayor of Blainville and former ADQ fundraiser Pierre Gingras. As he spoke, he had a list of *Le Téléjournal* headlines in hand. His objective was to demonstrate that Radio-Canada's coverage had been biased. His source was a list compiled by a Quebec City radio station that monitored the *Téléjournal* headlines for signs of an anti-Conservative bent, and was hell-bent on finding it. Let's just say that fans of this station were unlikely to be swayed by rational arguments.

The other director, Rémi Racine, had not yet been appointed chair at the time, but he was not going to be left out. Even if he was subtler, he still maintained that he had been "ashamed to watch the election night coverage on Radio-Canada."

During these interventions, President Lacroix said nothing. With a complicit air, he seemed to agree completely with his colleagues on the board. The message was clear. That is what I wanted to convey to my spouse when I told her, "It doesn't smell good ..."

Direct Links with the PMO

Above and beyond his good relations with James Moore, Hubert Lacroix was very open with his senior management about his great relationship with the prime minister's chief of staff, Nigel Wright. At least one memo published on the Radio-Canada website[18] shows that they occasionally had lunch together. Several sources have confirmed to me that this was not an isolated case. The two men saw each other several times over the course of 2011 and 2012.

According to my sources, they also exchanged regular phone calls in September, October, and November of 2011, during the negotiations around the implementation of the government's Action Plan to Reduce the Deficit (APRD).

They may have discussed other things. From what I have heard, Nigel Wright played a determining role in the government's decision to give Hubert Lacroix a second mandate as president of CBC/Radio-Canada in 2012.

Am I alone in thinking that it is abnormal for the president of CBC/

Radio-Canada to be in such close contact with the prime minister's chief of staff? I asked Lacroix's predecessor, Robert Rabinovitch, what he thought. He expressed some reservations:

> It's not normal, but it happens from time to time. I remember meeting with Jean Pelletier and [Eddie] Goldenberg[19] to discuss members of the board and in particular the performance of a member that I considered irresponsible.

He then added this, which I have previously quoted in Chapter 7:

> I never discussed programming with the PMO, nor the minister responsible for the CBC, and most were respectful enough not to raise programming issues....[20]

Let's recall that the former Progressive Conservative minister Marcel Masse had told us that he regularly met with the president of CBC/Radio-Canada at the time, Pierre Juneau, mainly to discuss the corporation's mandate. These discussions seemed quite normal to me, because at the time Masse was reflecting on amendments to the Broadcasting Act.

Of course it is important for presidents of the CBC to be able to talk to the political authorities, among other reasons to protect their budgets, but in my view they should always be aware of where their first loyalties lie. Should they devote themselves to the defence of the institution in their charge, or should they simply execute the orders of the governments that appointed them? One thing is certain — the fine balance in the relationship between politicians and the senior management of CBC/Radio-Canada depends on strong ethics on both sides.

Certain strong personalities have a better sense than others of the importance of setting boundaries. I believe that Pierre Juneau, Tony Manera, and Robert Rabinovitch are in this category. Happily, over the years, many vice-presidents and heads of News and Current Affairs have also been skilled at shutting down attempts at political interference.

A Poisoned Chalice

To return to the president's action plan to shake up the team around him: on July 20, 2011, Radio-Canada's ombudsman, Julie Miville-Dechêne, resigned.

Shortly thereafter, Minister Christine St-Pierre announced her appointment as president of Quebec's Council for the Status of Women. Stroke of luck for the president! He saw in this a way to pry me gently away from the leadership of News and Current Affairs.

On July 21, he mandated Sylvain Lafrance to offer me the position of ombudsman, to take effect immediately. Perhaps a bit boldly, I took the risk of declining the proposal, both because I wanted to continue my work as head of News and Current Affairs and, most of all, because I wanted to remain associated with the many investigative journalism projects I had under way. In fact, I very much wanted to stay where I was.

A few weeks later, on September 16, I received an intriguing phone call from an executive recruiter, inviting me to become the ombudsman. I respectfully reminded her that I had already refused the position and that I was passing on it at this time. An excerpt from my personal diary: "September 16th — call from V.K. for the position of ombudsman."

Another call from the recruiter, a week later: "You haven't changed your mind?" No.

She asked my advice about potential candidates. I suggested a few names, including that of the current ombudsman, Pierre Tourangeau.

In the meantime, the president was looking to fill another position: the vice-president of French Services. Louis Lalande had been doing the job on an interim basis since September 22, because of the departure of Sylvain Lafrance. He wanted the job, but Lacroix kept saying he wanted an outsider.

He had told Lalande this from the beginning. Several outsiders had been interviewed in September and October, notably Philippe Lapointe (who had been in several executive positions at TVA, Pixcom, and Transcontinental in addition to having previously worked at Radio-Canada) and Marc Blondeau (another former television executive who had also been at Rogers Publishing, now CEO of Place des Arts). The president had clearly announced his intention of making major changes. In early October, the president had his perfect candidate — a lawyer named Anik Trudel. He was all set to announce the appointment on October 3, but Trudel changed her mind when her existing employer, Edelman, offered her a major promotion. The whole process had to start over again.

To Broadcast or Not to Broadcast?

In October, I faced a serious dilemma. The team at our investigative flagship program *Enquête* told me they had a great story from reporter Julie Vaillancourt on the paving companies that were dividing up the contracts in the Lower St. Lawrence and Gaspé regions. "Bravo! But is there a problem?" I asked, seeing their worried faces.

"It's because one of the companies belongs to the president's in-laws." There was a long silence.

I had no choice. Important principles were at stake. If the information was true and in the public interest, we could not cover it up. In any case, that was not my style. And the *Enquête* team knew it. I gave my approval. "Make sure, though, that you have double- and triple-checked everything for accuracy. I don't want us vulnerable on a single detail!"

As it turned out, the investigators at the Charbonneau Commission also saw, as we had, matters that called for investigation.[21] I did not inform the president of the existence of this documentary in the production pipeline. I wanted to maintain my freedom until its broadcast, and at the same time I wanted to protect the team at *Enquête*. The report aired on October 13. On October 14, there are two notes in my personal diary.

The first says that I praised *Enquête* team at the weekly meeting of my department heads:

> October 14th — At the meeting of editors in chief, I emphasized the independence of Radio-Canada's journalists and the management of the News and Current Affairs Service, and the editorial freedom to broadcast on any subject matter, citing the *Enquête* documentary from the night before as an example.

The other note was more about myself. At 2:00 p.m., I was to meet Louis Lalande, the interim vice-president of French Services.

I had known him for a long time. We had been colleagues in senior management under Sylvain Lafrance, he in charge of the regions and I managing News and Current Affairs. He is tall, always a little nervous. He had worked in special programming in the 1980s; in 1992, he had even been my coordinating producer at *Le Point*. Later, he had left Radio-Canada to set up Le Canal Nouvelles, RDI's competitor. Upon his return, he had led Technical Operations, then Television News and Current Affairs in 2004. The journalists in the News and Current Affairs Service had always had trouble seeing Lalande as one of their own, which had been a career handicap for him. Some people believed that he had had it in for me since Sylvain Lafrance, when he was vice-president in 2006, had preferred me for the job of managing director of News and Current Affairs, all platforms. Personally, I had never felt that I was in competition with Lalande. I was in the habit of speaking to him frankly and directly. According to my personal notes, our October meeting unfolded no differently:

> October 14th —An "offer" from Louis Lalande at 2:00
> in his office: "Aren't you interested in the ombudsman
> job?" I have until Monday to decide.

In other words, he was pressuring me to reconsider my refusal to be a candidate for the job of ombudsman.

"Do you have a mandate from somebody to make me this offer?" I asked him at the time. What was I being reproached for? My investigations?

I was told no, the investigative stuff was great, what I was doing was very good. But things were going to be changing dramatically over the next few months. It wouldn't be easy.

I asked Lalande for his evaluation of the percentage of the chance that I'd be fired if I refused to be a candidate for the job of ombudsman. Knowing him, I was convinced that he would be evasive. Wrong! "Eighty percent," he said. At least things were clear.

I was almost devastated. It was Friday, and I had only until Monday to make my decision.

Let's be honest here. It's true that the job of ombudsman didn't much interest me, but I wasn't ready to despair. I needed a bit of time to evaluate three options. What were they?

One, accept being a last-minute candidate for the ombudsman position.

Two, resign and bring my retirement forward.

Three, pursue my work until the guillotine fell on me.

On Monday, I asked for a one-day extension to put together the information I needed to make my choice. I noted in my diary:

> October 17th — meeting with Louis at 9 a.m. in his office.
> Need another 24 hours to consult. Will let me know.

It was a long day, until the call from the interim VP in the late afternoon:

> October 17th — 5:38 p.m. – refusal to give me another
> 24 hours before declaring my candidacy for the job as
> ombudsman.

"What happens now, Louis?" I asked.

"I don't know, I really don't know."

I was left with only one option: wait to be fired. I had rejected the idea of resigning.

My last four months at Radio-Canada were like being on death row.

I took advantage of it to take stock of the last few years. I was proud of having surrounded myself with strong, talented executives, like Pierre Tourangeau as head of News, Luce Julien at RDI, and Jean Pelletier at Current Affairs. They were all part of my team, with the courage to broadcast what is sometimes very disturbing investigative journalism.

I continued to play my role actively, managing ongoing affairs and accompanying the investigative reporters in their work. I also blocked a few proposals from the sales department. In this respect, my job had become more arduous, because the thirst for revenues was pushing management increasingly in the direction of ignoring the rules laid out in CBC/Radio-Canada's Advertising Standards.[22]

Historically, these exemplary standards have allowed us to demand high levels of quality from sponsors and to protect the independence and credibility of our News and Current Affairs programming. In this way, Radio-Canada has led by example for decades and has certainly influenced the whole advertising industry. That era is unfortunately over. Over the last few years, new forms of advertising, more surreptitious and not always clearly identified, have suddenly become acceptable.

These changes have not escaped the eagle eye of former Radio-Canada host and former PQ minister Lise Payette, now a columnist at *Le Devoir*:

> In the old days, Radio-Canada would sometimes refuse sponsorships because their product was in bad taste or of insufficient quality, or because they featured a poor quality of French. Those days are over. One can advertise anything, anyhow, as long as you pay the big network price.[23]

Chasing revenues at all costs has created a situation in which advertising sales have taken television programming hostage. All my colleagues who are heads of programming areas know that the first among equals is the head of sales. We in programming are second-class citizens in this new world. If a program doesn't do well in prime time, its days are numbered. In my last two years at Radio-Canada, I had to fight several times to protect our international news show, *Une heure sur terre*, in its Friday 9:00 p.m. time slot. In the end, the show, hosted by Jean-François Lépine, was abandoned a year after my departure. Others will follow: under the intense scrutiny of the salespeople, their hour is coming. Even in program evaluations, revenues now prevail over the distinct role of a public broadcaster. Revenue is the new religion of the organization. The constant increase in commercial time clearly demonstrates this.

The new sales armada is supposed to save the public broadcaster. The result is that since 2012, French television revenues have increased by 33 percent, with advertising moving from twelve to fourteen — sometimes up to sixteen — minutes per hour. Just a few years ago, everyone was scandalized when commercial time was increased from eight to twelve minutes per hour. A two-minute increase in commercials within the nightly flagship newscast, *Le Téléjournal*, had also provoked a firestorm of protest.

In the management meetings I attended, I was openly scolded for being too concerned with ethics and not enough with raising revenues.

For example, I had refused to air an ad on behalf of Quebec's Federation of Medical Specialists that imitated the format of a news report to polish the image of specialist doctors.

This advertorial was supposed to be broadcast in the commercial breaks during *Le Téléjournal*. I felt the need to refuse to air the piece, because at the very same time there was an escalating conflict between the president of the federation, Dr. Gaétan Barrette (now Quebec's minister of health), and the Quebec government. Of course, it was entirely possible that *Le Téléjournal* would cover the story. Up to then, organizational ethics would always have allowed us to refuse to air political ads during the newscast. This rule remains crucial to the credibility of these programs.

Later, I was also reproached for refusing to allow a reporter to travel to Paris at the expense of Steven Spielberg's production company to attend the international launch of the 3D film *The Adventures of Tintin*. Such a trip clearly violated another golden rule, laid out in the CBC/Radio-Canada Journalistic Standards and Practices[24] as well as the Program Policies.[25] In my opinion, the ability to present news and current affairs report without sponsorship or advertising is fundamental to the reason for the existence of a public information service. I was able to keep my editorial freedom as head of a News and Current Affairs Service, but the internal environment was becoming more and more threatening.

At the same time, several people at the top of both CBC and Radio-Canada were also insisting that the News and Current Affairs Service participate in a mega-documentary to mark the centennial of the War of 1812.[26] This had become an important project for Minister of Canadian Heritage James Moore and Prime Minister Stephen Harper. In 1812, the United States had declared war against the British Empire over possession of Canadian territory. The Harper government felt that this war had played a central role in the affirmation of Canadian independence. Not all historians agree, notably in Quebec.

As head of News and Current Affairs, I refused to reallocate a portion of our budget to this operation, which had a whiff of propaganda about it.

Clearly, I was not the only media executive to see things this way. Here is what André Pratte, chief editorial writer at *La Presse*, had to say about it:

> What is worrisome here is that the Harper government takes these things to heart, as it has done in the case of symbols of the monarchy. It is legitimate to be concerned that the Conservatives will use a caricatural version of the history of the War of 1812 to "promote" Canadian nationalism for their own benefit.[27]

My personal stock was not going up here. However, in November 2011, *Enquête* swept the Judith-Jasmin Awards for excellence in journalism for its investigative reporting at the annual FPJQ convention. I was delighted! For me, this was the most valuable recognition of the work accomplished by Radio-Canada.

The Good Student

During this period, Hubert Lacroix was preparing a new wave of budget cuts.

In fact, from 2009 on, the president spent most of his time creating scenarios for cuts and reallocations. The first wave of cuts was a natural result of the economic crisis of the fall of 2009. In 2010, he hired Bain & Company, an international management consulting practice, to shuffle all the cards to reallocate money to fund his strategic plan for 2010–2015, *Everyone, Every Way*. All members of senior management had to make proposals to reduce spending in their areas of responsibility. French Services had to find $22 million in cuts to achieve the objectives of the strategic plan. Things got even worse in 2011–2012. This was because in the summer of 2011, the Treasury Board announced the implementation of the Action Plan to Reduce the Deficit, which would affect every department and agency, including CBC/Radio-Canada. The plan for Radio-Canada was due before March 31, 2012. There was pandemonium in senior management. A total of $115 million had to be carved out of CBC/Radio-Canada, of which $36 million was to come from French Services, $49 million from English Services, and $30 million from other sources, such as shutting down analogue transmitters and delaying real estate investments.

The palace guard around the president shared its objectives and its plans, but it was not alone. In the course of this exercise, Lacroix was in constant contact with the Prime Minister's Office and the bureaucrats in the Treasury Board.

According to my sources, Lacroix had already presented his detailed plan for budget cuts to Minister Moore in 2009, even before obtaining his board's approval. The same thing happened with the cuts linked to the APRD in 2012.

What is unique in this case is that the Treasury Board demanded minute details of what services would be cut, which productions would be affected, and even what programming decisions would be made. CBC/Radio-Canada had never prostrated itself in this way before the government of the day. The president was entirely cooperative throughout this process. For example, the Treasury Board was informed about the intention to introduce commercials on CBC Radio Two and Espace Musique to raise $20 million in additional revenues. Plans shared with the Treasury Board in advance indicated that precisely 43 permanent employees out of a total of 69 would be let go from Radio-Canada International and that production of content in Russian and Portuguese would stop. The plans also provided for an increase in commercial time on television from twelve to fourteen minutes per hour, which was to bring in an extra $40 million in new revenues. The devil is in the details. The $10 million fund for cross-cultural programming that allowed CBC and Radio-Canada to collaborate in the production of major documentary series such as *Love, Hate and Propaganda* disappeared — and nine jobs along with it. There is so much more, but the list is too long. Senior management provided so much information on the choice of possible cuts that the minister was able to give his opinion about each decision.

To my knowledge, CBC/Radio-Canada had never gone so far to share its intentions before implementing budget cuts. The Treasury Board undoubtedly pressed for the details, but the president did not seem to resist at all. It was unprecedented.

It got worse. Hubert Lacroix was a good boy, a well-behaved student, not only with the minister. His zeal extended to informing the Prime Minister's Office directly, on a weekly basis, about the preparation of the budget cuts. My sources tell me he spoke openly about the details in his weekly exchanges with the prime minister's chief of staff, Nigel Wright. Now that is truly unique!

A New Vice-President, Louis Lalande

The president was still searching for a vice-president of French Services to support his strategic plan. On January 12, 2012, he told us he had finally found the right person: "I was looking for an external candidate, without realizing that the rare gem was right here at Radio-Canada. Your new vice-president is Louis [Lalande]." The traditional applause followed.

According to my sources, invigorated by the withdrawal of Anik Trudel — the external "rare gem" candidate — the new vice-president, whose candidacy had been set aside early in the selection process, had relaunched his campaign. Obviously, as events would reveal, he had chosen compliance with the president's plans, executing everything he was asked to do. Including firing the head of News and Current Affairs.

On February 22, 2012, I was summoned to the office of the new vice-president, who told me that my association with Radio-Canada was ending here and now. There were going to be major changes, and I was no longer part of his plan, he said. Even though I had been expecting it, it was a shock all the same, accompanied by grief. The next day, early in the morning, I finished drafting my internal memo to staff, which included the following sentences:

> I am sorry to be leaving you in such turmoil, but know that it is not by my own choice. Since 1984, I have devoted my life to sustaining the institution that is Radio-Canada. It is a unique and invaluable jewel.... I have always tried to exercise free and independent leadership, as I am a free man with values to defend.

A memo from the vice-president announcing my departure from management was released around the lunch hour. Lalande underlined that under my leadership "... investigative journalism has made remarkable headway and built a high profile, creating a real impact in the social and democratic lives of our fellow citizens."

This came as a shock to the staff in the Centre d'information (the news centre for radio, television, and RDI staff, known as the CDI). Very few people were aware of the quiet machinations that had been under way for many months.

Three union representatives came to my office to find out more about what was going on. One of them broke down in tears — and so did I.

"Do you intend to call a staff meeting?" they asked. I did not feel capable of it. I simply told them that I would publish my personal memo to staff at 3:00 p.m. Only then would I come down to the CDI to greet them, and no more.

At 3:00 p.m., I went down, my memo in hand. What followed was completely unexpected, and entirely memorable. As soon as I appeared, dozens of people gathered around me, some launching a wave of applause that seemed never-ending.[28] From the corner of my eye, I could see the on-air anchor for RDI, Michel Viens, who wanted me to come and explain the reasons for my departure to the audience. I refused. Staff members were arriving in the newsroom in wave after wave. I was told afterwards that the elevators were jammed full of people coming down from the tower towards the lower level, where the CDI was located, and that senior management was watching nervously as the events unfolded live to air from the CDI.

"It's better to see this much affection while you're still alive than at the funeral parlour," I joked through a veil of tears.

An employee of the News Service was brave enough to write to the president to protest my firing. In the answer that he sent her, Lacroix denies all responsibility. It is worth reproducing his reply here (in which he uses the informal *tu* rather than the formal *vous*):

> I have read your note. You are entitled to your opinion. But I have a question for you: why are you writing to me about this? Do you really think I choose the Managing Directors who work in French Services? Don't you think you should have the guts to speak directly to Louis [Lalande]? Cheers.

The following week, I was invited to the popular Sunday night round table talk show program *Tout le monde en parle* (*Everybody's Talking About It*). I declined the offer, because I truly did not know how to explain things. In hindsight, I can talk about what happened with greater knowledge, because I know a lot more about the facts behind the decision.

The truth is that part of the president's plan had just been implemented. I was aware that I represented the opposition inside management. I was against an exercise that seemed to me to distort the very concept of public service, and I always expressed my opinions frankly, defending those principles and the same values. I know that others continue to fight, even today, and they have all my respect.

A Renewed Mandate

After a few months of frequent exchanges with Nigel Wright and jumping to attend to James Moore's slightest wish, Hubert Lacroix finally got what he wanted. He won. On October 5, 2012, the minister announced his renewal for another five-year mandate as president of CBC/Radio-Canada.[29] This was a first. In the past, a few presidents have had one- or two-year extensions, but never a complete five-year mandate renewal.

This time, it was clear that Wright had played a determining role. Someone else had also influenced the decision: the chair of the board, Rémi Racine. He was satisfied and let it be known to his colleagues:

I have the pleasure of announcing that the Honourable James Moore, Minister of Canadian Heritage and Official Languages, has today confirmed the reappointment of Hubert T. Lacroix for a second five-year mandate as President and CEO of CBC/Radio-Canada, excellent news for Canada's public broadcaster. One thing is certain: the Board has unanimously supported Hubert's reappointment. This renewal is a vote of confidence for Hubert and supports our 2015 strategic plan: Everyone, Every Way [www.cbc.radio-canada.ca/fr/decouvrez/strategies/strategie-2015], as well as our leader's vision to express our culture and enrich our democracy.[30]

Don't Touch the Brand

In June 2013, James Moore denounced Radio-Canada's decision to change its name and to start calling itself ICI. Tampering with the Radio-Canada brand is risky. Previously, in 1995, under Prime Minister Jean Chrétien, senior management had wanted to change the name, especially to get rid of the word *radio*, which is no longer very representative of the corporation's range of activities. It had chosen the abbreviation SRC, to be consistent with CBC and to conform to the pattern of using three letters, as most of the world's great television networks do.

The change had been proposed by Robert Patillo, vice-president of communications at the time. The moment was ill chosen. The country had just been through the most recent referendum, and Jean Chrétien was still upset about the tight outcome. He had accused Radio-Canada of having done a poor job of "defending Canadian unity."

Management had been under a lot of pressure through some of the intermediaries on the board, then chaired by Guylaine Saucier. The public broadcaster was accused of trying to remove the word *Canada* in its name; some interpreted this as a separatist plot. My sources say this pressure was coming straight from the government.

The vengeful attitude of the Liberal government was in the air. The name "Radio-Canada" remained, and the Canadian flag subsequently appeared on all the satellite dishes.

In this case, the question was not whether or not it was a good idea to replace the brand or the name "Radio-Canada" with "ICI". It was that the attempt to do so had opened the door to a political intervention by the minister.

Here was the sequence of events: In January 2013, senior management of French Services presented its rebranding project to the board, chaired by Rémi Racine. It was approved and applauded. Hubert Lacroix then reversed himself completely. The minister of Canadian heritage saluted this reversal: "Our position is very clear, it is that the perception of Canada must be very clear in the branding of the network. It's very important for us," he declared.[31]

Radio-Canada certainly took a hit in public opinion and managed to convey the impression that the minister was in the driver's seat.

I am not contesting the federal government's right to choose the name of the institutions that come under its authority. I am simply remarking on the fact that the politicians believe it is essential to have the word *Canada* in the name of the French network while it is just fine for the English network to represent Canada with a single initial in the CBC logo (rather than the full Canadian Broadcasting Corporation). This is why I speak of political interventions.

In the meantime, Radio-Canada television continues to bear its anachronistic name.

Wave after Wave of Cuts

Since my departure in the spring of 2012, Hubert Lacroix has continued to implement the objectives of the Conservative government. He has reduced the size of the public broadcaster and is proceeding to dismantle it and to dilute its relevance.

In 2012, the president announced a second wave of cuts: $115 million related to the Action Plan to Reduce the Deficit. Then there was a third wave in April 2014. This time, it was $130 million, requiring the loss of 657 jobs, 312 of them in the French network.

Barely three months later, on June 26, 2014, he tabled his strategic plan for 2015–2020, which projects the retirement of another 2,500 people. The great dismantling is in progress. To console the threatened employees, the best Radio-Canada offered was to provide the services of a psychologist and an employment counsellor.

Of course, it is important to look modern. The president is proclaiming everywhere that he wants to make the transition to digital at top speed. He even expressed "great pride" — his words — in announcing his plan to his senior executives on a telephone conference call. He achieved the pinnacle of the art of disguising bad news as good news. But no one was fooled.

Since the start of 2014, the president has been increasingly taken to task, both in public and inside the organization, where he has lost all sympathy or benefit of the doubt that the staff may have expressed towards him in the early days. Many have denounced his complicity with the views of the Harper government, which dislikes both Radio-Canada and CBC. This reaction is founded, given the extent of the disaster.

Here is a direct and articulate criticism by Francine Pelletier, columnist at *Le Devoir* and former reporter and producer at both Radio-Canada and CBC:

> In other words, Mr. Lacroix seems to worry more about the "ecosystem" of broadcasting than about the magnificent animal of which he is the guardian, concentrating more on what has to be cut to obey the authorities than on what must be done to save, not just the furniture, but the very soul of Radio-Canada.[32]

Nevertheless, Lacroix enjoyed the support of the minister of Canadian heritage, Shelley Glover, who had this to say about the most recent strategic plan:

> As an arm's-length Crown corporation, CBC/Radio-Canada is responsible for its own operations, including strategic planning of this nature. As with all Crown

corporations and Government agencies, we encourage CBC/Radio-Canada to take advantage of new and more efficient ways of doing business. [33]

CHAPTER 11

The Great Dismantling

One wonders why the Conservatives dislike Radio-Canada. At the origin of their negative attitude, of course, we can find their basic political ideology. In fact, they simply do not see the relevance of having a public broadcaster, because they believe that private enterprises meet the same needs for radio and television.

The party believes that government must be as little involved as possible in competing with the private sector, which is the principal motor of the economy.

In some ways, the Harper government had the same perspective on Radio-Canada as the Liberal governments of Pierre Trudeau and Jean Chrétien. All of them saw it as simply a nest of leftists and sovereigntists. With Stephen Harper, this perception was compounded by the Conservative preference for the smallest possible role of the state.

That being said, Harper's government, a bit like that of Trudeau before him, behaved as if it were the sole proprietor of Radio-Canada. The difference is that, from the time of their assumption of power, the Conservatives behaved like owners who wilfully neglect their property and leave it to deteriorate until the only option is to tear it down.

In addition, the Conservatives sought to avoid debate on the matter as much as possible — somewhat like the abortion issue. Most of them were opposed to abortion, but the prime minister did not want to rock the boat.

So he let a few of his people deploy their strategies. For the public broadcaster, the chosen policy was laissez-faire and slow asphyxiation

— and it was an astute one. Other observers also evoked this scenario, particularly Lise Payette: "But Stephen Harper will continue to cut. Unless he decides to sell it to private enterprise. He is entirely capable of it."[1]

The hypothesis was not farfetched. Remember that the sale of CBC and Radio-Canada Television was part of former Reform MP Jim Abbott's[2] plans. Many other Conservative MPs have openly supported the idea of dismantling the CBC and Radio-Canada.

We are not quite there yet, because the government preferred to avoid a public debate. But in the meantime, the asphyxiation strategy is slowly working. If there ever is an eventual sale, it could be done piecemeal.

Lacroix Executes the Dismantling Scenario

Budget cuts have long been part of the public broadcaster's history. Remember that in 1995, President Tony Manera resigned in protest against the cuts.

It is clear that such an idea has never crossed Hubert Lacroix's mind. In April 2014, he absorbed the third series of major budget cuts since his arrival in office while avoiding as much as possible any criticism of the government.

And it is not over, as we can see in his most recent five-year strategic plan focused on the transition to digital,[3] released in June 2014, which presages a true haemorrhage.

If he were a skilled strategist, the president would have found a way to put the facts before the public and the politicians to provoke a debate both in public and in Parliament, before proceeding to the haemorrhage stage. That is not the path that he has chosen. He did not want to displease the government. He preferred to follow the preordained plan to dismantle the place.

It is true that mass public indignation has not shown up in any obvious way, as Marc Cassivi pointed out in *La Presse* on April 22, 2014:

> The new cutbacks, far from raising public indignation, are taking place in quasi-general indifference. The public broadcaster is being bled before our eyes and we are

watching it in prolonged death throes without making a fuss about it. As if maintaining high-quality television and radio programming and national and international news and current affairs coverage worthy of the name had not the slightest importance to us. [4]

How to explain this relative apathy? I have read no studies on the subject, but I can put forward a personal hypothesis: the current surfeit of media and sources of information and the illusion that what is digital is free make it more difficult to identify content as coming from the public broadcaster.

This content seems to be a tiny piece of what is available, diluted in digital space, not rooted in territory or nationality. How then, under these conditions, can we understand its importance and its relevance?

In contrast, however, Hubert Lacroix's unveiling of the 2015–2020 strategic plan provoked a firestorm of protest among the employees and those who believe that the public broadcaster will remain just as relevant, if not more so, in the digital era.

In June 2014, during the teleconference to launch the plan, a CBC union representative dared to call the president a facilitator for those who want to destroy the institution. The president answered him: "What do you want me to do? I have no choice." The employee's response was scathing: "You could protest and resign."

Such reactions are not surprising. The strategic plan, *A Space for us All*, has been rejected by all. Why? First of all, because it is a mess, a glib, lazy piece of work with senior management surfing on a few bits of modish jargon.

The people who really understand the situation at CBC/Radio-Canada are all uncomfortable with the document — among other reasons, because it is clear that there has been no due diligence with regard to the long-term financial projections. In reality, it is not a strategic plan at all, but rather a mass layoff plan disguised as a strategic plan. It proposes a continuous downsizing over five years. It is blindingly obvious that the real objective is to reduce the size of the corporation by getting rid of 2,500 employees! The digital transition is simply a decoy.

In the document, senior management admits that television advertising revenues have hit their limits. There must therefore be another way to compensate for the continuing reduction in government revenues. For starters, the idea is to chase Internet advertising revenues, while admitting that this will not be easy. Then there is talk of selling most of the real estate assets, merging as many services as possible, and migrating radio music programming and television in the smaller markets to the Internet.

What is striking is that, aside from letting staff go, nothing in the plan is quantified. Management is content to say that the digital transition will save a lot of money and that it hopes to succeed in doing this. There is a tendency to assume that digital costs almost nothing, and it is true that on the television side, these technologies can perform virtual miracles. However, the stiff competition in this area can also require major investments. The websites that are currently sustainable are the work of giants in the field whose fiercely competitive offerings draw on very deep pockets. Unless there is a major change of direction, there is very little chance that CBC/Radio-Canada will have the necessary resources to carve out a privileged place in this market. This is so obvious that even the authors of the strategic plan admit it discreetly:

> In addition, these Internet-created corporations have unprecedented size and access to funds that allow them to make long-term, strategic investments. The space reserved for Canadian voices is more fragmented; the ongoing competition for audience attention puts more pressure than ever on CBC/Radio-Canada to ensure its relevance to the Canadian public.[5]

The risk with this plan is that the speed with which the corporation must realize these savings and dig up entirely new revenue streams precludes orderly implementation of the necessary changes. The future seems to hold nothing but excruciating death throes under the watch of an indifferent government.

The plan contains another surprising element. It is premised on the idea that CBC/Radio-Canada's mission has been amended. The public broadcaster's responsibility for democratic life and culture has been simply edited out.

Here is the description of the mission in the 2010–2015 strategic plan:

> In pursuit of our mission to express Canadian culture and enrich the democratic life of this country, we strive to be a socially minded organization in everything that we do.[6]

And here is the new definition of CBC/Radio-Canada's mission the strategic plan for 2015–2020:

> CBC/Radio-Canada expresses Canadian culture and enriches all Canadians through a wide range of content that informs, enlightens and entertains.[7]

Quite a difference!

But let's return to the mindset that led to the creation of this plan. Already in May 2014, the president was showing his true colours at a hearing of the House of Commons Standing Committee on Official Languages:

> In 2020, we need to be a smaller and more focused public media company, one that is more agile and can adjust as the media consumption habits of Canadians change.[8]

Yvon Godin, the NDP MP for the minority-language constituency of Acadie-Bathurst, peppered Lacroix with withering criticism, accusing him of fatalism rather than fighting for the rights and needs of minority language communities.

"It is not fatalism. It is an observation," Lacroix replied, sealing the perception of the president as a cold, unengaged bystander rather than the defender and champion of the public broadcasting mission we would have hoped to have in a time of crisis for the institution.[9]

CBC/Radio-Canada, One Company

One thing that Hubert Lacroix — and the chair of the board, Rémi Racine — will defend passionately is the idea of managing CBC and Radio-Canada as a single enterprise without distinguishing between the two services. We should not forget that Lacroix does have some expertise — in the business of mergers and acquisitions. Had he not said to each of his two vice-presidents, Sylvain Lafrance and Richard Stursberg, that he did not understand their respective roles under his presidency?[10]

In the introduction to the 2015–2020 *A Space for us All*, the CEO explained himself on this subject: "Working as one company, by 2020, we will be smaller in size but more effective and more focused."[11]

This, then, is Lacroix's other objective: to bring together the majority of the services in the two language groups under one management. This is the end of Radio-Canada's autonomy inside the corporation, as Raymond David always defended it. We can even speak of a negation of the history of the two distinct language groups in Canada. Management of French Services is losing the financial latitude to develop a distinct strategy, adapted to the needs of the francophone audience.

The result of implementing this idea is to treat Radio-Canada and CBC as equals in every respect, despite their specific differences.

Here is the story behind the adoption of the notorious strategic plan *A Space for us All*. On June 16, 2014, the CEO sat down with Minister of Canadian Heritage Shelley Glover to share his plan with her and to try to obtain funding to facilitate the departure of many employees to retirement by offering them settlements. She was to provide him with an answer in the following days.

He tabled the plan with the board at its June 16–17 meeting. It was approved, pending assistance from the minister with the budget attached to it. On June 20, the minister replied that she would not be helping the corporation to finance the transition to digital.

On June 24, at the very last minute, the sixteen pages of the strategic plan were sent for emergency translation to French without any regard to adapting the differences relevant to the reality at Radio-Canada. In "one company," it was to be expected. The enormous pressure of the last-minute request resulted in a very awkward French translation. Hence, "The vision is the aspirational goal" became "Notre vision est le but ambitieux"[12] which makes no sense in French. The document was presented to the staff a day and a half later, on June 26.

The starting point for the 2015–2020 strategic plan is the performance of CBC rather than that of Radio-Canada. CBC Television attracts something like 8 percent of anglophone audience share in prime time. Radio-Canada's French television service is far ahead of that, at more than 15 percent of francophone audience share in prime time, with peaks of more than 20 percent in the fall of 2013.

It is possible that CBC Television's audience share will fall even more with the loss of the rights for *Hockey Night in Canada* to Rogers. The least we can say about this arrangement is that it is unusual. Most of the games now appear on the Rogers property Sportsnet, and Rogers receives all advertising revenues for NHL hockey games in Canada. Under a four-year deal, CBC continues to broadcast the Saturday night games. CBC does not pay for the production of the games and it has no editorial control over the broadcasts, but neither does it receive any of the revenues from these broadcasts.

Whatever the outcome, Lacroix's strategic plan should have taken into account the differences between the two networks to avoid throwing out the baby with the bathwater. Lacroix's previous assignments had involved teaching securities law and mergers and acquisitions law at l'Université de Montréal's faculty of law. Merged businesses are his area of expertise. "It's a single business," he told Anne-Marie Dussault, who was interviewing him on the RDI program *24/60* on April 10, 2014.

And he hastened to add that the historically protected share of the budget for each of the two networks — 60 percent for CBC and 40 percent for Radio-Canada — was "a myth." This led me to write in a paper for *Le Devoir* on April 14, 2014: "So the distinct character of the French Services has been ended without any announcement to that effect?"[13] In fact, it was the first time that the two networks generated equal commercial revenues, despite the fact that the French network is four times smaller than the English network. Ironically, this successful performance by the French network was used to wipe out the deficit of the English network.

Even the English-language media became aware of this. In July 2014, the *Globe and Mail*'s Konrad Yakabuski wrote an article headlined: "Don't Make Radio-Canada Subsidize the CBC", setting the record straight:

> As the cuts keep coming, fans of Radio-Canada, one of the most watched public broadcasters anywhere, are starting to resent paying the price for the CBC's failure to connect with Canadians. That resentment is likely to grow as the broadcaster faces an ongoing cash crunch and slashes 1,500 more jobs by 2020. With the loss of Hockey Night in Canada, the only CBC program to consistently deliver big ratings, advertising revenues at the English network risk sinking below those brought in by the French side, which draws millions more viewers despite operating in a much smaller market.[14]

This "one company" vision also had a major impact on management. From the beginning, the new president had attached value only to those initiatives that were integrated between the two entities.

The joint meetings multiplied along with newly created committees and sub-committees; in other words, the opportunities to exchange with our anglophone colleagues started to grow.

This also had consequences for the language used in meetings. The absence of bilingual managers on the CBC side meant that English was always the favoured language. If a francophone executive were to speak French in a meeting, it required the presence of simultaneous interpreters. This seemed to irritate the president, because it slowed meetings down and, in his eyes, made them less efficient. The result was that our joint meetings with CBC meetings unfolded increasingly in English and that francophones never had a choice in the matter. Not surprising that the strategic plan had been conceived in English. That is often what one company means.

In the summer of 2014, an external firm was hired to propose a major structural reform of CBC/Radio-Canada. The English and French sales teams had already been merged under a single management in the spring of 2014. The rumour is that the next groups to be merged will be in finance. This threatens to end the tradition of protected budgets for the French network. There is also talk of merging program services. If that were to happen, it is reasonable to fear for all the creative and cultural aspects of French programming.

Focus on Content

From the telegraph to the digital era, and through radio and television, the world of communications has existed only to transmit content. In general, public broadcasters have been different from other content producers at every step of technological evolution.

There is no reason for us to be bamboozled today by the plumbing and the platforms of the digital era. We have to master them, of course. But what distinguishes a public service will always be its content. In that sense, CBC/Radio-Canada's strategic plan should always give priority to the creation of distinctive content that can subsequently be adapted to a new environment. Of course we need to adapt the structure of production and make it more flexible, but first and foremost with the goal of supporting and spreading CBC/Radio-Canada's unique expertise. The strategic plan is remarkably silent on the way to maintain high-quality production that is not submitted to commercial imperatives on a smaller budget. I also note that in this era of globalization and growing complexity, the plan does not even mention the importance of international news and current affairs. It only mentions helping Canadians talk to other Canadians. It offers us the perspective of becoming more insular. Not such a great plan!

The New Digital World Era

The new technological, financial, and political environment is so disruptive that the 2015–2020 strategic plan must be submitted to a far more rigorous due diligence. It is time to review the very definition of CBC/Radio-Canada and the description of it in the 1991 Broadcasting Act. But it is out of the question to change the nature of the country's most important large cultural and democratic institution without involving both parliamentarians and the public. The turmoil in the media that has come with the digital era cries out for a public debate. A refusal to do this simply removes the institution from much-needed democratic validation.

Let us agree that the idea is not to be nostalgic or overly rooted in our personal memories. The objective is not to go back to the past.

Given the speed of current change, all media have to constantly bring their strategic plans back to the drawing board. Few can predict what will remain of traditional radio and television in a few years. Young people are cutting the cord and abandoning traditional television. Consumption habits are rapidly changing.

A recent U.S. study[15] nevertheless demonstrates that people watch more television than ever, but at a time of their choosing. The most likely scenario is that the future belongs to television content on all the current platforms and some that remain to be invented.

Even major Hollywood stars such as Kevin Spacey are moving away from the big screen and towards digital content for television; he stars in *House of Cards*, which was commissioned by online distributor Netflix. Young people have been quick to adopt these changes. They love having the latest content, which they exchange on social media, and being the first to find the most innovative sites. These young people know that they can choose the time and manner of their media consumption. They have tamed the future. And here we are pushing them out of the future of public broadcasting, since they are the first to be laid off. Such a strategy is dramatically and dangerously mediocre. Radio-Canada needs to respond to these new expectations with its own public broadcasting content — which is never defined in its strategic plan. But to attempt to do it without the participation of young people is utterly nonsensical. In the meantime, it is also an imperative to design a real transition plan that is attentive to the needs of the older audience, which is not yet ready for the digital transition.

We will always need to be wary of the futurologists. The death of radio was announced decades ago, and it is now very much alive on all platforms. And the end of television? It too is very much alive, also on all platforms, at every hour of the day. It is certainly much too soon to sign its death warrant.

CBC/Radio-Canada's Relevance in the Digital Era

When CBC/Radio-Canada was first created, as we saw in Chapter 1, it had to counter the power of the American presence on the airwaves and to invest in Canadian culture and democracy to serve anglophone and francophone citizens well. At the dawn of television, the goal was the same. Since the earliest days of the Internet, that goal has been more important than ever.

Today we need solid benchmarks, free and independent strongholds against, among others, those whom author and expert Éric Scherer calls the "new predators":

> a handful of web giants, armed with their unprecedented power and their dominant position, seem invincible. They are fragmenting and locking down the web, which was to be a free space.[16]

The role of the public broadcasting service is precisely to counter those who want to control the democratic space, those who want to "lock down the web" and attempt to standardize public ideas and culture.

One doesn't have to be paranoid to fear the powerful multinationals that control the digital space and dictate the rules of the game.

In 2014, Google had 53,600 full-time employees. And what is Google's mission? Here is what the company says on its website: "Google's mission is to organize the world's information and make it universally accessible and useful."[17]

I don't find that very reassuring.

You don't have to be paranoid or delusional to fear that specialists and manipulators will analyze our personal, cultural, and — why not? — political profiles on social networks.

Already in June 2014, we found out that Facebook had conducted a secret experiment on 700,000 users without their consent. In the light of the information on Facebook user profiles, the study's authors found that their emotions were contagious. From there to emotional manipulation for commercial or possibly political ends seems like a small step.

Here are a few comments on the Facebook experiment published on June 30, 2014, in the Paris daily *Le Figaro*, quoting an article from an American scientific publication:

> Reading positive statuses makes us feel good. To see our friends depressed puts us in a bad mood. And a flow of neutral news leads us to post less on Facebook. These conclusions are not really surprising, but the method of their compilation is problematic. Many U.S. commentators were indignant that the study, which they feel approaches mental manipulation, was conducted without the consent of web users.[18]

Of course, we have the good fortune to live in a democracy. We are not subject to a totalitarian regime that looks to uncover and destroy the sources and places of dissidence. Nevertheless, I feel enormously uneasy knowing that governments, businesses, or organizations can spy on my slightest actions on social networks without my knowledge, often with the complicity of the owners. Democratic societies have always been suspicious of illegal wiretapping, and we must have the same standards for digital spying.

The current challenge remains cultural and democratic. Still, many voices have been raised to denounce the powerful tentacles of the new digital players.

Here is another commentary by Éric Scherer about Edward Snowden's revelations on the large-scale spying in the digital world:

> What a rude awakening! Once betrayed, is trust lost? In the new information era, the public is starting to be infected by doubt and anxiety about the place of these double-edged-sword technologies in our lives: they are formidable tools for knowledge, communication and

simplification, but they have also become dangerous informants to governments and multinationals who now know our habits, behaviours and activities.[19]

These are examples that should convince us to push for strong, free, and independent public information services. There have to be some remaining players who can watch and critique the excesses and abuses of these new giants.

Already in 2006, at a conference of the European Broadcasting Union, its legal counsel, Werner Rumphorst, wrote in a piece titled "How to guarantee the independence of public service television?"

> In conclusion, we must fight to have independent public service broadcasting, but once this independence is a given, we will have to defend it firmly against those who would attack it openly or through the back door. [20]

When I was in charge of News and Current Affairs, there were many accusations and pressures from all sides, and I often had to reaffirm the independence of the service for which I held responsibility. I understood the need for constant vigilance. This is one of the reasons why I insisted so firmly on including the protection of our independence in the introduction to the Our Mission and Values section in the revised version of CBC/Radio-Canada's Journalistic Standards and Practices. Here is the result:

> We are independent of all lobbies and of all political and economic influence. We uphold freedom of expression and freedom of the press, the touchstones of a free and democratic society. Public interest guides all our decisions. [21]

The current senior management of CBC and Radio-Canada has, unfortunately, failed at this task. It is up to all of us to re-establish, firmly, the independence of the public broadcaster.

Is a Multimedia Public Service Still Relevant?

Yes! Public enterprises like CBC/Radio-Canada are the best service to offer Canadian citizens. The relationship of trust established over the years must continue into the digital era for all of us. Nevertheless, the transition to digital technologies offers the opportunity to redefine what a public broadcaster has to offer in this new era.

What to do with CBC/Radio-Canada when it is becoming harder to discover in a universe that offers billions of Internet sites? This raises three kinds of problems:

First, we do not face a lack of information. The current problem is an overabundance of information!

Second, real information shares the web with disinformation, which is more and more invasive in this digital era.

Third, we are all victims of attempts to manipulate us, which provokes a serious crisis of trust towards digital information among those who are most aware of the danger.

It is important to acknowledge that the critical mindset is not widespread enough. As I always tell my journalism students: information versus disinformation is the extreme battle of the twenty-first century.

In this battle, our first reflex is to hope that the public broadcaster can play a major role in the distribution of local, regional, national, and international information. Obviously, by this I mean real journalism, with enough resources to present well-researched reports and investigations.

I have previously referred to my creation of *Enquête* and the assembly of a team of high-impact investigative journalists at Radio-Canada as two of my good decisions as head of News and Current Affairs. These decisions are often cited in defence of Radio-Canada and in appeals to support it.

In a world where, more than ever, the media business model is based on advertising revenues to enrich mega-businesses that are taking up more and more economic space, we need a free and independent source of information. In fact, CBC/Radio-Canada must no longer define itself as a series of platforms (radio, television, Internet, and mobile). The objective is to preserve the accumulated knowledge and skills to produce high-quality content and to distribute it in the digital universe. In news and current affairs, the corporation has to develop a brand that is immediately identifiable as the source of public information in Canada and available to all in a digital environment. The formats have to be varied and adapted to all new devices. Above all, the content must always be distinctive because it has been produced while respecting CBC/Radio-Canada's fundamental values.

What is true for a specialized sector such as CBC/Radio-Canada's News and Current Affairs must also be true of its dramas, its entertainment, and its sports programming.

Comedy programs such as *This Hour has 22 Minutes* on CBC and Radio-Canada's famous year-end parody show, *Bye-bye*, must always enjoy the freedom to make fun of events and people in the news. The corporation will always attract criticism, but it is worth both the effort and the cost involved.

In drama series, the boldness of a public broadcaster can be seen in productions that depict nonconformist and avant-garde characters and plots. It is important to have the ability to take risks and to address any subject, even those that may offend the ideological sensitivities of groups and political parties.

These days, there is no need to prove that there are attempts to standardize cultures and ideas. The Hollywood executives are masterful at the art of blasting out their cultural universe. It is the responsibility of the public broadcaster to fight this trend toward standardization and to offer diversity as an alternative option.

With regard to culture, it is important to counter the power of the cultural multinationals and to offer creators a space in all disciplines. Cultural content that is off the beaten path, which is produced by emerging talent — these are areas where the public service broadcaster has a niche.

Even in the area of sports journalism, it is important to develop an approach to offer independent sports news and current affairs. When the same people own both the media outlets and the sports teams, this is bound to restrict the freedom of that outlet's journalists. There again, free and independent journalism is on the public service side.

Finally, the richness of a democratic society such as ours lies precisely in the power to think critically. Private broadcasters tend to offer a simplistic discourse on societal issues. In a way, we can understand that this is easier to sell. But it means that there is little room on these networks for intellectuals, who are labelled ivory tower thinkers. And yet, in such a complex society, it is important to offer a substantial, diversified, and subtle take on the issues.

To man the ramparts against monolithic thinking, that is a great and beautiful challenge for a public broadcaster!

CBC/Radio-Canada's history is marked by this openness to the world, to cultures and ideas. This is a form of wealth for all Canadians, and particularly for francophones, since they form a minority in North America.

Opposing the Dismantling

For the last few years, we have had the impression that CBC/Radio-Canada is like a train, derailing at top speed and headed for a wall. Powerless and fatalistic, citizens are indifferent, as if the collision were inevitable.

But we can avoid this catastrophe.

The future of CBC and Radio-Canada cannot be left solely in the hands of its senior management and the government. The debate must be taken to Parliament. It is imperative to develop a new Broadcasting Act for the digital era. Everyone — civil society, individuals devoted to the public interest, media experts, democrats, and all political parties — must have a chance to express themselves on this subject.

Any new law must make CBC/Radio-Canada a public service (and not a state service) for the digital era. This law must recognize the distinctive characteristics of content and programming for francophones and for anglophones. It must specify that the two services are distinct, in order to serve the linguistic communities effectively in Quebec and across Canada.

In fact, there should be two legal enterprises, one for anglophones and one for francophones.

A new law must also include clear guarantees of arm's-length status to keep a healthy distance from political power. The method of appointing presidents for the two networks must be reviewed and corrected to submit the chosen candidates to a hearing before a committee of Parliament. This procedure should also apply to appointments to the boards of the two entities.

These positions must be the subject of public posting and transparent selection criteria, to be defined and applied.

The CBC/Radio-Canada act for the digital era should be the subject of a broad public debate, with the participation of the CRTC and beyond the regulatory agency as well. The public service is indeed a "space for us all," to paraphrase the June 2014 strategic plan.

Finally, it is important to understand that this is an urgent matter. A bit like family and civic values, ethical standards and ways of practising journalism and making programs have to be handed down from one generation to the next. We cannot allow a whole generation of young people, ready to take up the profession, to disperse. Nor can we afford to let the significant emotional attachment to the CBC/Radio-Canada brand that has accumulated over the decades go to waste. Marketing experts will tell you that to build or to rebuild attachment to a brand takes an enormous amount of time and effort, especially once strong competition is already in place. We must handle this precious, intangible legacy wisely.

Three Sources of Financing

With regard to funding CBC and Radio-Canada, I believe we should rely on three sources.

First, we should have stable government funding over a five-year period. Second, we should have a device-based royalty inspired by the European models. Third, we should keep an open mind about commercial revenues, but we should cap them somewhere between 15 and 20 percent of the overall budget.

The royalty model is well established in most European countries, where the amount is payable on the purchase of devices that can display or record television programming. For other kinds of devices, the model varies by country. But this kind of formula has the advantage of sheltering the public broadcaster from the whims of the government of the day as it puts together its annual budgets.

It may also be time to explore what contributions the government requires from the web-based multinationals that are gobbling up the audiovisual market, thanks to the spread of smart phones and tablets. With the CRTC, it is also time to examine what CBC/Radio-Canada should be able to extract from those same multinationals, whose new devices rely heavily on public broadcasting content to supply their own services: Apple, Google, Microsoft, and others. (With regard to this, governments around the world, not just Canada's, need to take up the cudgel of cultural diversity with these giants.)

In the end, it will be necessary to keep a portion of government funding if we want to finance CBC and Radio-Canada separately, i.e. to guarantee a distinct envelope for French and English services.

Obviously, the level of this funding needs to ensure the viability of the new public entities and allow them to escape the dictatorship of ratings and the endless search for commercial revenues. We have seen how these factors can influence content. The public broadcaster will always need the capacity to offer clearly distinctive programming and content.

Let's get to work!

CONCLUSION

What became of my friends, whom I held so close and loved so much?

— "Pauvre Rutebeuf"

Every time there is bad news — and unfortunately, the flow never seems to stop — I think right away about my friends who are still employed at Radio-Canada. How are they doing under the circumstances, these people who are among my greatest professional friendships? As the poem "Pauvre Rutebeuf" opens: "What became of my friends, whom I held so close and loved so much?" I continue to experience the painful feeling of watching such an essential institution deteriorate before my eyes.

Today, the sadness and lack of motivation have reached a point where many of CBC/Radio-Canada's most valued employees are leaving, or are thinking of doing so. In September 2014, Radio-Canada television lost its highly regarded managing director, Louise Lantaigne, who resigned after having instigated such great successes as the drama series *Unité 9* and *Série noire*. There would be other departures, because very few people internally believed that the new strategic plan would actually create a better future.

Are there really only a few of us who are so deeply worried about the future of CBC/Radio-Canada? Is it not time to stop asphyxiating the public broadcaster?

I share a great passion with my friends and colleagues at Radio-Canada: working for the public's right to high-quality information and cultural programming.

We always said that Radio-Canada would never die, that it would survive all the changes of government and management. We were wrong.

Conclusion

We thought that the culture of its artisans was stronger than anything that could be thrown at them and would guarantee the long-term survival of the institution. That was a mistake. CBC/Radio-Canada can die. Increasing numbers of us are watching it being dismantled, sometimes as co-conspirators and sometimes with indifference. Others are totally helpless and don't know what to do to reverse the decline.

Of course, the public broadcaster is not perfect. Its programming is not always exemplary. However, it has certainly contributed to enriching our democracy and our culture. It is not Radio-Canada's past that we need to preserve; it is its future that we need to protect and build in a society and a world that are increasingly complex and difficult to decode.

I cannot reconcile myself with the idea of living in a society where all information and culture is strictly a consumer product. Mercantilism must not dictate the relationships among people. In order to avoid this outcome, we need to preserve democratic institutions that are driven not solely by profit, but also by meaning.

The digital era carries great hope for building knowledge and skills. In this new era, democratic life holds immense challenges. In every country where they exist, public service broadcasters — radio and television networks as well as their digital extensions — have made major contributions to democracy, politics, society, and culture. The public broadcaster can accompany citizens as this new society emerges.

In this book, I have described the evolution over the years of the specific relationship between CBC/Radio-Canada and the government of the day, through changes of government and direction.

I believe I have demonstrated how difficult it is to find the right balance in the relationship between the two parties.

It is true that the public broadcaster is under government jurisdiction. It may be natural that those in power have a tendency to behave as if they owned the place, but this tendency must be fought. The public broadcaster serves the people, not the government, and must not be transformed from a public service into a mouthpiece for the state. The so-called owner is a stand-in for the people — all the people — not a direct owner. That is the price of democracy.

On the other hand, CBC/Radio-Canada must learn to live with the government of the day by establishing clear boundaries. Preventing governments from interfering with programming and with policy decisions about the organization's direction and management is vital and fundamental.

In conclusion, I want to emphasize that the original French title of this book, *Ici était Radio-Canada*, putting the traditional Radio-Canada on-air identification into the past tense, was not a wistful attempt at nostalgia. Rather, my hope is to write the next chapter of this history, one of a CBC/Radio-Canada that will have adapted to the modern world and that enjoys stable, long-term funding so it can continue to serve the people.

APPENDIX

Memo from Alain Saulnier to News and Current Affairs staff:

February 23rd, 2012

Louis Lalande has decided to proceed with the transformation of News and Current Affairs with someone other than myself. This is his legitimate right. I will therefore be leaving Radio-Canada on March 16th.

I am sorry to be leaving you in such turmoil, but know that it is not by my own choice.

Since 1984, I have devoted my life to sustaining the institution that is Radio-Canada. It is a unique and invaluable jewel. I am very proud of the career that I have had here and of what I have accomplished.

As I look back, I believe I have launched a great momentum for investigative journalism, motivated by my profound belief in democracy. As a journalist, I have always been convinced that institutions, governments and organizations must operate under rules of transparency and equity for all. I believe deeply in equality of opportunity.

Since I have been in charge of News and Current Affairs, I have also made room for a lot of international coverage, as I am convinced that we, the francophones of this country, should participate actively and proudly in opening up to the world and its critical issues.

I have always pushed for the highest quality of coverage. All subject matter should be on the table to be covered, but in our own way, as a public service broadcaster should do it. What is the point of public broadcasting news and current affairs if it looks like what everyone else is doing? I am also proud of having pushed our organization to create specialized teams in our major coverage areas, thereby demonstrating our uniqueness in the francophone media world.

I have always tried to exercise free and independent leadership, as I am a free man with values to defend.

At the FPJQ, through our Guide de déontologie [Code of Ethics], and here, in my daily practice and with the adoption of the new Journalistic Standards and Practices, my professional life has been profoundly committed to ethics. This is consistent with my conviction that rectitude, integrity and responsibility are essential values for us.

My management style has always been based on respect for others. I have always decried the authoritarian, disrespectful style of management. My admiration for the work we do is too great to not respect everyone who works here, and those who have worked at my side.

Finally, I have been able to rely on a fantastic team, even if it has not always been easy! I have always thought that it is best to be surrounded by strong people if we want to move forward.

Radio-Canada is fortunate to be able to count on such deeply engaged people.

Thank you,

Alain

NOTES

Introduction

1 *Pépinot et Capucine* was the first children's television show broadcast by Radio-Canada, from 1952 to 1954 and then in repeats. The characters were puppets.

2 All well known characters from Radio-Canada's first children's television shows.

3 Excerpt from Article 35 of the Broadcasting Act, Chapter 11: "This Part shall be interpreted and applied so as to protect and enhance the freedom of expression and the journalistic, creative and programming independence enjoyed by the Corporation in the pursuit of its objects and in the exercise of its powers."

Chapter 1: Beginnings

1. Jacques-Narcisse Cartier was also influential in the development of a pan-Canadian radio network. He presented a brief to the House of Commons entitled *Le Rôle véritable de la radio dans la vie d'un people* (*The True Role of Radio in the Life of a People*).

2. Dupont was later to found CJAD, whose call letters were based on his initials.

3. Pierre Pagé, "La radiodiffusion 1922–1997" ["Broadcasting's 75th Anniversary"], *Fréquence/Frequency*, nos 7–8 (1997): 54.

4. Pierre Pagé, *La première décennie de CKAC (1922–1933)*. Une radio privée dans l'esprit d'un service public, créée par Jacques-Narcisse Cartier, Phonothèque québécoise, Musée du son, www.phonotheque.org/radio/ckac.html.

5. Alain Canuel, "La censure en temps de guerre: Radio-Canada et le plébiscite

de 1942" ["Censorship in Wartime: Radio-Canada and the 1942 Plebiscite"], *Revue d'histoire de l'Amérique française*, vol. 52, no 2 (Autumn1998): 217–242.

6. Norman McLaren was born in Scotland in 1914 and died in Montreal in 1987. A producer at the National Film Board, he was considered one of the world's greatest film animators. More information here: http://blog.nfb.ca/blog/2011/12/01/70-years-of-animation-part-2-norman-mclaren/.

7. See http://www.cbc.ca/archives/categories/arts-entertainment/media/radio-canadainternational-canadas-voice-to-the-world/rene-levesque-reports-from-korea.html.

8. *Rue principale* was one of Quebec's first radio soaps. It was on the air for twenty-two years, with plots ranging from love stories to mysteries. It was scripted by a series of writers, first Édouard Baudry, then Rolland Bédard, Paul Gury, and René O. Boivin. It was broadcast by CKAC, CHRC, and Radio-Canada.

9. *Un homme et son péché* was first a novel by Claude-Henri Grignon. It became a radio series in 1939. The main character's name was Séraphin Poudrier.

10. This game show aired on Radio-Canada television from 1958 to 1966. When contestants answered the host's questions correctly, they could choose between a modest cash prize or an egg containing a prize of unknown value.

11. A late-night comedic talk show that could be described as an ancestor to *Appelez-moi Lise* and *Tout le monde en parle* on Radio-Canada television.

Chapter 2: Temporary Difficulties

1. *Opération mystère* was the very first science fiction show for kids at Radio-Canada.

2. *Prise de bec* (which could be translated as *Spat*) was one of the first shows devoted to political debate. Hosted by Roger Duhamel, it aired from 1956 to 1958. See the Fond Roger Duhamel, BAnQ Vieux-Montréal.

3. Gérard Filion, "Plusieurs ministres du gouvernement Duplessis ont commis un délit d'initié en achetant des titres de l'entreprise québécoise de gaz natu-rel avant leur émission" ["Several Ministers in Duplessis's Government Trade as Insiders, Buying Pre-Issue Shares in Quebec's Natural Gas Company"], *Le Devoir* (June 13, 1958).

4. Jean-Pierre Desaulniers, professor in the faculty of communications at UQAM, died in 2005. He conducted many studies of Quebec television.

5. Quoted in Véronique Robert, "50 ans de télé" ["50 Years of Television"], *L'actualité* (August 2002).

6. Ibid.

7. FPJQ press release, February 1992.
8. Radio-Canada's fiftieth anniversary series, Radio-Canada Archives.
9. Jean Duceppe was the father of Gilles Duceppe, leader of the Bloc Québécois.
10. Roux also served as a Senator from Quebec and Lieutenant-Governor of the province.
11. Gérard Pelletier had been a journalist, commentator, and union leader before becoming a minister in the Liberal federal government of Pierre Trudeau.
12. The two interviews are part of a series of programs especially for Radio-Canada's fiftieth anniversary.

Chapter 3: The End of the Monopoly, the Beginning of Tensions

1. *Capitaine Bonhomme*, later *Le Zoo du capitaine Bonhomme*, starred its original creator, Michel Noël.
2. *La Boîte à surprises*, broadcast from 1956 to 1972, starred a number of memorable characters for children of that era: Fanfreluche, le Pirate Maboule, Michel le Magicien, Grujot and Délicat, Sol and Gobelet, etc.
3. Fanfreluche was a doll brought to life by actress Kim Yaroshevskaya, who told stories and legends that she could enter and modify as she wished (1968–1971).
4. Université de Sherbrooke, "Inauguration du poste de télévision Télé-Métropole" ["Inauguration of the Télé-Métropole television Station"], Bilan du siècle, bilan.usherbrooke.ca/bilan/pages/evenements/20153.html.
5. My entire message to employees is reproduced in Appendix I.
6. Of course, the question is also relevant to Radio-Canada's cultural sector, but in a different way.
7. The Public Broadcasting Service (PBS) is an American television network that is non-governmental and non-profit, financed by its subscribers and through its perennial public fundraising campaigns. Its programming policies focus primarily on childhood education, broadcasting major cultural events, and documentaries. *Maclean's*, November 1966.
8. *Maclean's (français)*, November 1966.
9. The Royal Commission on Bilingualism and Biculturalism was co-chaired by André Laurendeau, editor-in-chief of the daily newspaper *Le Devoir*, and Davidson Dunton, president of Carleton University. Often called the Laurendeau-Dunton or the B&B Commission, it was created by the Pearson government in 1963.
10. In the short film *Les Vacances d'Elvis Gratton* (*Elvis Gratton's Vacation*), Elvis Gratton tries to explain his identity to a French person: "I'm a Canadian-Québécois; a French-Canadian; a French North American; a

Québécois-Canadian francophone; a Québécois of French-Canadian-French expression. We are Canadian-American francophones from North America; we are Franco-Québécois."

11. Quoted in Denis Monière, *Le Développement des idéologies au Québec* [*The Development of Ideologies in Quebec*] (Montreal: Québec Amérique), 1977.

12. First elected in the 1965 federal election, Pierre Elliott Trudeau was first parliamentary secretary, then minister of justice, before becoming prime minister.

13. *Séparatiste*: the preferred word of the "Trudeauites" to describe those who preferred to describe themselves as *indépendantistes* and *souverainistes*.

14. Pierre Elliott Trudeau, *Le Fédéralisme et la société canadienne-française* [*Federalism and French-Canadian Society*] (Montréal: HMH, 1967), 203.

15. East of Quebec, the Acadians tend to celebrate August 15 instead.

16. Claude Jean Devirieux, *Derrière l'information officielle, 1950–2000* [*Behind the Official Information, 1950–2000*] (Québec: Septentrion, 2012).

17. Broadcasting Act, 1968 wording. Broadcast scholar Marc Raboy has explained that this difference in wording was because what English Canadians had no problem considering "Canadian identity" could not be easily rendered in French, where the reality was seen as a dual Canadian identity.

18. Benoît Lévesque and Jean-Guy Lacroix, "Les libéraux et la culture: de l'unité nationale à la marchandisation de la culture 1963–1984" ["The Liberals and culture: from national unity to the merchandising of culture 1963–1984"], in Yves Bélanger et al., *L'Ère des libéraux: Le pouvoir federal de 1963 à 1984* [*The Liberal Era: Federal Power from 1963 to 1984*] (Montréal: Presses de l'Université du Québec, 1988), 257–293. The article is available at: classiques.uqac.ca/contemporains/levesque_benoit/liberaux_et_la_culture/liberaux_et_la_culture.html.

19. The quotation "mettre la clé dans la boîte" is accurate, but the expression is not the usual formulation. Trudeau presumably meant "lock it up and throw away the key." Elsewhere in the same speech, he repeated the same expression, but stopped and added "in the door."

20. Radio-Canada, Format 30, October 21, 1969, archives.radio-canada.ca/emissions/261/.

21. Radio-Canada, Format 30, October 20, 1969, archives.radio-canada.ca/politique/premiers_ministres_canadiens/clips/14791/.

22. Prime ministers of Canada who preceded Pierre Trudeau.

23. Claude Ryan, "La colère intempestive du prince," *Le Devoir* (October 22, 1969): 4.

24. Pierre Pagé, *Histoire de la radio au Québec* [*The History of Radio in Quebec*]

(Montreal: Fides, 2007), 159.

25. Raymond David, "Grandeurs et misères du journalisme électronique" ["The ups and downs of electronic journalism"], speech to the Richelieu Club, December 1969, Radio-Canada Publications.

Chapter 4: A Collision of Identities: From the October Crisis in 1970 to the Election of the Parti Québécois in 1976

1. Marc Thibault, internal memo, March 10, 1977.
2. "Les médias et la crise d'Octobre" ["The Media and the October Crisis"], *Le Point* (October 10,1990).
3. Ibid.
4. Claude Ryan, "Les mesures de guerre : trois questions" ["The War Measures: Three Questions"] *Le Devoir* (October 17, 1970).
5. Excerpt from the 1968 Broadcasting Act quoted in the 1968 edition of Radio-Canada's Politique journalistique (Journalism Policy).
6. Marc Raboy, *Occasions ratées : Histoire de la politique canadienne de radio-diffusion* [Missed Opportunities: A History of Canadian Broadcasting Policy] (Montréal: Liber, 1996), 240.
7. In the 1968 version, the word "imposed" was replaced by "decreed."
8. Radio-Canada, *Politique journalistique [Journalism Policy]* (1982), 95. Author's emphasis.
9. Benoît Lévesque and Jean-Guy Lacroix, *Les libéraux et la culture* (Montréal: Les Presses de l'Université du Québec), 119–123.
10. Letter from Prime Minister Pierre Trudeau to the chair of the CRTC, March 4, 1977. Quoted in the CRTC report *Rapport du Comité d'enquête sur le service national de radiodiffusion* [*Report of the Committee Investigating the National Broadcaster*] (July 20, 1977): V.
11. CRTC, *Rapport du Comité d'enquête sur le service national de radiodiffusion*.
12. Jacques Hébert and Pierre Elliott Trudeau, *Deux innocents en Chine rouge* [*Two Innocents in Red China*] (Montréal: Éditions de l'Homme, 2007 [1961]).
13. The expression "Quebec nation" is in quotation marks in the report.
14. Speech to the Empire Club of Toronto, December 1, 1977, http://speeches.empireclub.org/61627/data.
15. Graham Fraser and Ivor Owen, *René Lévesque and the Parti Québécois in Power* (Montréal: McGill-Queen's University Press, 2001), 129.
16. "L'information au réseau français de Radio-Canada" ["Information at the French network of Radio-Canada"], conclusion of a presentation to a CRTC hearing, October 5.

17. CESTI: Centre d'études des sciences et techniques de l'information.
18. Claude Jean Devirieux, *Manifeste pour le droit à l'information: De la manipulation à la législation* [*Manifesto for the Right to Information, from Manipulation to Legislation*] (Montréal: Presses de l'Université du Québec, 2009), 48.
19. André Payette, telephone interview with the author, April 24, 2014.
20. Mario Cardinal was head of news from 1970 to 1974, mostly on the television side. He also worked for many years in print and as a journalist and producer at Radio-Canada. He was Radio-Canada's ombudsman from 1983 to 1989. He is the author of several books, including *Il ne faut pas toujours croire les journalistes* [*You Shouldn't Always Believe Journalists*] (Bayard Canada, 2005) and *Point de rupture, Québec/Canada: Le référendum de 1995* [*The Breaking Point, Quebec/Canada: The 1995 Referendum*] (Bayard in collaboration with la Société Radio-Canada, 2005).
21. Mario Cardinal, telephone interview with the author, April 28, 2014.
22. Réal Barnabé, email to the author, April 29, 2014.
23. Paul Larose, email to the author, May 20, 2014.
24. Sophie Thibault, telephone interview with the author, May 26, 2014.
25. Jean Giroux, telephone interview with the author, June 2014.
26. Marc Thibault, "L'Information au réseau français de Radio-Canada" ["Information at the French network of Radio-Canada"], a presentation delivered in Ottawa on October 5, 1978, published by Radio-Canada Public Relations, 9.
27. The Commission of Inquiry into the Sponsorship Program and Advertising Activities, chaired by Mr. Justice John Gomery.

Chapter 5: Pierre Trudeau Promises Change

1. Raymond David, personal notes from March 20, 1979, to February 23, 1982.
2. Raymond David, interview about his vision of Radio-Canada, June 24, 1965 [archives.radio-canada.ca/arts_culture/medias/ clips/17288/].
3. Michel Roy was the Associate Editor of the newspaper *Le Devoir* at the time.
4. Francis Fox was then minister of communications.
5. Francis Fox, interview with the author, September 11, 2014.
6. Ibid.
7. The word *putsch*, literally a plotted revolt or attempt to overthrow a government, comes from the German for violent blow or clash and came to mean "coup" in standard German and Swiss popular uprisings of the 1830s. In its

use during the Racine incident, it was clearly related to the impression of Marc Thibault as "God the Father" versus impatient young men anxious to take the reins of power for themselves.

8. Paul Racine, telephone interview with the author, June 8, 2014.
9. Ibid.
10. Paul Racine, telephone interview with the author, June 19, 2014.
11. Paul Racine, telephone interview with the author, June 18, 2014.
12. Francis Fox, interviewed September 11, 2014.
13. Sophie Thibault, telephone interview with the author, May 26, 2014.
14. Marc Laurendeau, "Les journalistes de Radio-Canada. La grève prend de l'ampleur mais sans encore secouer la torpeur" ["Radio-Canada's journalists. The strike broadens without shaking up the torpor"], La Presse, November 15, 1980.
15. Louise Cousineau, "Paul Racine nie être putschiste" ["Paul Racine denies being a putchiste"]. *La Presse*, November 27, 1980.
16. Two other Ottawa correspondents at the time.
17. Paul Racine, telephone interview with the author, June 19, 2014.
18. Réal Barnabé, email to the author, April 26, 2014.
19. Paul Racine, telephone interview with the author, June 19, 2014.
20. Francis Fox, interview with the author, September 11, 2014.
21. It's impossible to say whether Raymond David's diary erred on the date or whether President Johnson had obtained a copy of the editorial the day before its publication.
22. Michel Roy, "Black-out à Radio-Canada" ["Black-out at Radio-Canada"], editorial, *Le Devoir*, November 26, 1980.
23. Ibid.
24. Michèle Lasnier was a host at Radio-Canada, where she had once worked with Jeanne Sauvé.
25. Jeanne Sauvé was minister of communications from December 1975 to June 1979. At the time when this note was written, she was the Speaker of the House of Commons.
26. Paul Racine, telephone interview with the author, June 20, 2014.
27. Marc Thibault subsequently chaired Quebec's Press Council from 1987 to 1991.
28. Madeleine Poulin, email, June 12, 2014.

Chapter 6: 1984 — Marcel Masse and Pierre Juneau

1. Francis Fox, *Building for the Future: Towards a Distinctive CBC*, September 1984.

2. Francis Fox, interview with the author, September 11, 2014.

3. Fox, *Building for the Future*, point 6, "A merchandising role for the CBC."

4. Ibid., point 4, "Role with regard to national unity."

5. Francis Fox, interview with the author, September 11, 2014.

6. Florian Sauvageau, interviewed on the occasion of the death of Pierre Juneau, Radio-Canada archives, February 21, 2012.

7. This and the following quotes are from the author's interview with Marcel Masse, June 3, 2014.

8. Broadcasting Act, 1968.

9. Broadcasting Act, 1991, Article 3.

10. Later on, from 2004 to 2010, the same Richard Stursberg was vice-president of CBC's English-language services.

11. Richard Stursberg, email of May 27, 2014.

12. Pierre O'Neil, internal memo, November 6, 1989.

13. André Ouellet and Marc Lalonde were senior ministers under Pierre Trudeau.

14. Réal Barnabé, email to the author, April 26, 2014.

15. Supreme Court of Canada judgment of December 15, 1988, regarding the use of languages other than French in public and commercial signage in Quebec (known as the Ford judgment). Ford vs. Quebec (Attorney-General) [1988] 2 R.C.S. 712. The Supreme Court concluded that the ban on the use of languages other than French on public and commercial signs violated freedom of expression. The Court nevertheless left the door open to requiring clear predominance of the French language.

16. Pierre O'Neil, internal memo, January 12, 1989, 4:35 p.m. EST.

17. "Robert-Guy Scully quitte le journalisme" ["Robert-Guy Scully leaves journalism"], Radio-Canada, June 9, 2000, [ici.radio-canada.ca/nouvelles/49/49328. htm]. See also excerpts from Mario Cardinal's book *Il ne faut pas toujours croire les journalistes* [*You Shouldn't Always Believe Journalists*] (Bayard Canada, 2005), published in *Le Devoir*: www.ledevoir.com/non-classe/74475/ les-derapages-de-l-information-l-affaire-lester-une-affaire-de-deontologie-ou-de-politique.

18. Jean-François Lépine, interview with the author, May 22, 2014.

19. Marcel Masse, interview with the author, June 3, 2014.

20. Ibid.

21. Florian Sauvageau is a professor of journalism at Laval University. Gerald Caplan is a historian who was an Ontario candidate for the New Democratic Party in the 1982 election.

22. Florian Sauvageau, email to the author, June 3, 2014.

23. Gerald L. Caplan and Florian Sauvageau, *Report of the Task Force on*

Broadcasting Policy, Ottawa, Supply and Services Canada, 1986.

24. This major part of the report, unfortunately, was shelved.

25. Florian Sauvageau, email to the author, June 3, 2014.

26. E. Kaye Fulton, interview with Tony Manera. Fulton wrote: "Only later did the president make his reason clear. 'I will not preside over the dismantling of the CBC,' Manera told *Maclean's*." http://www.encyclopediecanadienne.ca/fr/article/cbc-president-manera-resigns-en-anglais-seulement/

27. Paul Racine, telephone interview with the author, June 20, 2014.

28. Ibid.

29. "The Juneau Report, a good thing for Radio-Canada," FPJQ news release, January 31, 1996.

30. Lise Bissonnette, "Pour une vraie télévision publique" ["For a real public television service"], *Le Devoir*, February 2, 1996.

31. Mario Cloutier, "Radio-Canada doit fuir la propagande" ["Radio-Canada must shun propaganda"], *Le Devoir*, February 2, 1996.

Chapter 7: From One Referendum to Another

1. Renaud Gilbert, interview with the author, February 18, 2014.

2. Alain Saulnier (president of the FPJQ), letter to the editor, *La Presse*, July 20, 1992.

3. Jean Bédard was a political reporter at RDI.

4. At the time, Liza Frulla was the Liberal MNA for Marguerite-Bourgeois in the National Assembly.

5. Free translation of the French version of a document for which the English version is unavailable.

6. Pierre Jomphe served in News and Current Affairs management under Claude Saint-Laurent.

7. Claude Saint-Laurent, telephone interview with the author, January 21, 2014.

8. Telbec, Release #300,095, 4:03:34 p.m., October 27, 1995.

9. Liza Frulla, interview with the author, June 11, 2014.

10. Claude Saint-Laurent, telephone interview with the author, January 21, 2014.

11. Quoted by Chantal Hébert, "Ottawa declares war on Radio-Canada", *La Presse*, November 14, 1995.

12. Paule Des Rivières, *Le Devoir*, November 14, 1995, 1.

13. Hugh Windsor, the *Globe and Mail*, November 14, 1995.

14. Courtesy of Friends of Canadian Broadcasting.

15. Robert Rabinovitch, email to the author, June 3, 2014.

16. With the latest Harper budget cuts, the CBC's parliamentary grant will fall to a new low of $29 per capita.

17. Al Johnson, Pierre Juneau, Tony Manera, and Laurent Picard, the *Globe and Mail*, January 25, 1997.

18. Ibid.

19. Claude Saint-Laurent, telephone interview with the author, January 21, 2014.

20. Ibid.

21. Pierre Gravel, "De nouveaux vases chinois" ["Chinese Vases, Again"] editorial, *La Presse*, November 18, 1998.

22. Graham Fraser, "Fear and Loathing for the CBC," the *Globe and Mail*, April 10, 1999.

23. The Office of the Ombudsman, French services, Radio-Canada, Montreal, March 19, 1999.

24. Al Johnson, Pierre Juneau, Tony Manera, and Laurent Picard, *La Presse*, January 25, 1997.

25. Mario Roy, "SRC, l'heure des choix" ["CBC, Time to Make Choices"], editorial, *La Presse*, October 20, 1999.

26. Antonia Zerbisias, "CBC's New Chief Wins Top Ratings All Around", *Toronto Star*, October 19, 1999: A1.

27. Robert Rabinovitch was appointed deputy minister of communications by Francis Fox. He held the position from 1982 to 1985.

28. Antonio Zerbisias, "CBC's New Chief Wins Top Ratings All Around".

29. Robert Rabinovitch, email to the author, February 23, 2014.

30. Edith Cody-Rice, *CBC and the Arm's Length Relationship*, File #2006-00023, 28. The document was obtained through Access to Information.

31. Edith Cody-Rice was at that time CBC/Radio-Canada's senior in-house legal counsel.

32. Gérard L. Caplan and Florian Sauvageau, *Report of the Task Force on Broadcasting Policy*, Ottawa, Minister of Supply and Services, 1986: 263.

33. Ibid, 285.

34. Edith Cody-Rice, *CBC/Radio-Canada and the Absence of the Arm's Length Relationship*, 15.

35. Pierre Trudel, *Le Pouvoir du gouvernement d'exiger des plans et de donner des directives à la CBC/Société Radio-Canada* [*The Government's Power to Demand Plans and to Give Directives to CBC/Radio-Canada*], April 3, 2005: 5. The document was obtained under Access to Information legislation. For the full text, see CBC and co. v. R., [1983] 1 S.C.R. 339.

Notes

Chapter 8: From One Government to Another

1. Liza Frulla, interview with the author, June 11, 2014.
2. Standing Committee on Canadian Heritage, *Our Cultural Sovereignty, The Second Century of Canadian Broadcasting*, Ottawa, 2003: 624, 624, and 635 [www.parl.gc.ca/content/hoc/committee/372/heri/reports/rp1032284/her-irp02/herirp02-e.pdf].
3. Jim Abbott, Canadian Alliance Dissenting Opinion, Standing Committee on Canadian Heritage, June 2003: 843.
4. Bev Oda was transferred to the ministry of international cooperation in 2007 after she was found to have incurred travel expenses that were considered to be excessive.
5. Paul Cauchon, "Radio-Canada est dans la mire des conservateurs" ["Radio-Canada in the Conservatives' cross-hairs"], *Le Devoir*, April 21, 2006.
6. Christine St-Pierre, letter to the editor, *La Presse*, September 7, 2006.
7. Bernard Drainville was a host and reporter at Radio-Canada. He was elected as a Parti Québécois member of the National Assembly for Marie-Victorin in 2007, 2008, and 2012; he was named to Pauline Marois's cabinet in September 2012 and subsequently ran unsuccessfully for the leadership of the party.
8. Pierre Duchesne was a reporter covering Quebec's National Assembly for Radio-Canada. He ran under the Parti Québécois banner and was named minister of higher education in Pauline Marois's government in September 2012.
9. Raymond Archambault was a reporter/anchor on Radio-Canada's radio newscasts. He was defeated as a Parti Québécois candidate, but subsequently became president of the party.
10. Stephen Harper, speech to the Economic Club of New York, September 10, 2006, [http://www.pm.gc.ca/eng/news/2006/09/20/speech-economic-club-new-york].
11. Dany Bouchard, "Plainte de Stephen Harper: à Radio-Canada, on fait le mort ..." ["Stephen Harper's complaint: Radio-Canada Plays Dead"], *Le Journal de Montréal*, January 25, 2007 [fr.canoe.ca/divertissement/tele-medias/nouvelles/2007/01/25/3445862-jdm.html].
12. The team was made up of reporter Guy Gendron, producer Jean-Luc Paquette, and researcher Monique Dumont.
13. Dimitri Soudas was a most arrogant press secretary. Experienced parliamentary journalists can testify to that. In an odd turn of events, Soudas has now become a Liberal.
14. Michael Fortier was a senator and minister in the Harper government from February 2006 to September 2008. He resigned from the Senate in

September 2008 to run as a Conservative candidate. He was not elected, which ended his political career.

15. Daniel Gourd was vice-president of French Television from July 2002 until November 2005.

16. Under the law, the appointment is submitted for the approval of the Governor in Council. The Broadcasting Act, article 36 (2): "There shall be a Board of Directors of the Corporation consisting of twelve directors, including the Chairperson and the President, to be appointed by the Governor in Council."

17. Broadcasting Act, article 40: "The Corporation is ultimately accountable, through the Minister, to Parliament for the conduct of its affairs." It should be noted that Parliament is a broader forum than the government.

18. Letter from Robert Rabinovitch to Hubert T. Lacroix, president-designate, November 13, 2007. The letter was obtained through an Access to Information request. The full document is available in Appendix III.

Chapter 9: The Lacroix Style

1. The new president referred constantly to CBC/Radio-Canada (his way of amalgamating the English and French Services) and never solely to Radio-Canada without including the initials CBC. However, the broadcaster uses only CBC in the English text and only Radio-Canada in the French text.

2. Broadcasting Act, 1991.

3. See Jean-François Cloutier, "Le patron de Radio-Canada cumule les fonctions" ["Radio-Canada Boss Holds Several Jobs"], *Argent*, January 11, 2012, [argent.canoe.ca/nouvelles/affaires/le-patron-de-radio-canada-cumule-les-fonctions-11012012].

4. Fibrek inc. vs. Abitibi Bowater (Produits forestiers Résolu), QCCQ1745, March 9, 2012; QCCA 569, 27 mars 2012; Autorité des marchés financiers, April 4, 2012. The case ended up before the Supreme Court in December 2012.

5. "Purge complète chez Fibrek" ["Complete purge at Fibrek"], *Argent* (Affaires), May 10, 2012 [argent.canoe.ca/nouvelles/affaires/purge-complete-chez-fibrek-10052012].

6. See *La Presse* canadienne, "Les ex-dirigeants de Fibrek se sont partagé 8,2 millions avant de démissionner" ["The former management of Fibrek split $8.2 million among themselves before resigning"], *Le Devoir*, May 31, 2012 [www.ledevoir.com/economie/actualites-economiques/351246/les-ex-dirigeants-de-fibrek-ont-obtenu-8-2-millions-avant-de-demissionner]. "Former Vice Presidents Patsie Ducharme (Finance), Dany Paradis (Procurement), Jean-Pierre Benoit (Sales and Operations) and Emmanuelle Lamarre-Cliche (Legal

Affairs) all received payments between $671,931 and $914,157."

7. Jean-François Cloutier, "Le patron de Radio-Canada cumule les fonctions."

8. He had left the position in April 2008.

9. See Chapter 8 for more details.

10. CBC, Journalistic Standards and Practices, "Our Values", [http://www.cbc.
radio-canada.ca/en/reporting-to-canadians/acts-and-policies/programming/
journalism/].

11. Friends of Canadian Broadcasting, "Conservative Broadcasting Corporation",
news release, April 30, 2013 [www.friends.ca/press-release/11380].

12. Philippe Mercure, "Rémi Racine, président d'A2M: de la politique aux tueuses
à gages" (Rémi Racine, President of A2M: from politics to female hired killers),
La Presse, April 12, 2008 [affaires.lapresse.ca/economie/200901/06/01-685601-
remi-racine-president-da2m-de-la-politique-aux-tueuses-a-gages.php].

13. Quoted in ibid.

14. Brian Myles, "Commission Charbonneau — Gilles Cloutier implique un
juge de la Cour supérieure" ["Charbonneau Commission — Gilles Cloutier
implicates a Superior Court Justice"], *Le Devoir*, May 2, 2013 [media2.ledevoir.
com/politique/quebec/377185/commission-charbonneau-des-dons-illegaux-
pour-avoir-les-contacts-necessaires].

15. Pierre-André Normandin, "Tecsult faisait du financement illégal au
provincial" ["Tecsult Was Making Illegal Contributions in Provincial
Politics"], *La Presse*, May 22, 2013 [www.lapresse.ca/actualites/dossiers/
commission-charbonneau/201305/22/01-4653111-tecsult-faisait-du-
financement-illegal-au-provincial.php].

16. Yves Poirier, "Cité à la commission Charbonneau le ministre Moore enquête
sur Pierre Gingras" ["Quoted at the Charbonneau Commission — Minister
Moore investigates Pierre Gingras"], *TVA Nouvelles*, May 23, 2013, [tva-
nouvelles.ca/lcn/infos/national/archives/2013/05/20130523-140649.html].

17. Simon Boivin, "Direction de l'ADQ: Christian Lévesque courtisé" ["ADQ
Leadership: Christian Lévesque being courted"], *Le Soleil*, June 2, 2009
[www.lapresse.ca/le-soleil/actualites/politique/200906/01/01-862000-di-
rection-de-ladq-christian-levesque-courtise.php].

18. Privy Council Office, "About the Privy Council Office" [http://www.pco-
bcp.gc.ca/index.asp?lang=eng&page=about-apropos].

19. Pierre Trudel, interview with the author, March 28, 2014.

20. Bill Chambers, then vice-president for branding, communications, and
corporate affairs, CBC/Radio-Canada, memo, December 2, 2010.

21. "Alumni Profile — Alfred McLeod", The Australia and New Zealand School
of Government, March 24, 2011 [www.anzsog.edu.au/blog/2011/03/147/
alumni-profile-alfred-mcleod].

22. Bill Chambers, then vice-president for branding, communications, and corporate affairs, release, May 31, 2013.
23. Bill Chambers, memo to staff, CBC/Radio-Canada. Free translation of the French version of an unavailable English-language original.
24. Treasury Board Secretariat of Canada, "Assets and Acquired Services" [http://www.tbs-sct.gc.ca/aas-gasa/index-eng.asp].
25. Bill Chambers, memo to staff.
26. Radio-Canada, "Radio-Canada/CBC supprimera 657 emplois en deux ans" ["CBC/SRC Will Eliminate 657 Jobs Over Two Years"], April 11, 2014, [ici.radio-canada.ca/nouvelles/societe/2014/04/10/006-radio-canada-compressions-lalande-lacroix.shtml].
27. Radio-Canada, *Un espace pour nous tous* [www.cbc.radio-canada.ca/_files/cbcrc/documents/explore/transforming/un-espace-pour-nous-tous-v12-fr.pdf].
28. Radio-Canada, "Marc Bellemare vide son sac" ["Marc Bellemare gets things off his chest"] April 13, 2010 [ici.radio-canada.ca/nouvelles/politique/2010/04/12/004-bellemare-entrevue.shtml].
29. James Moore was in this position from October 2008 to July 2013.
30. Stéphane Baillargeon, "La série Hard est retirée de Tou.tv" ["The series Hard is removed from Tou.tv"], *Le Devoir*, March 8, 2012 [www.ledevoir.com/culture/television/344524/la-serie-hard-est-retiree-de-tou-tv].
31. Hubert T. Lacroix received the email from James Moore at 12:34 p.m. on June 29, 2011. Three minutes later, at 12:37 p.m., he forwarded it to the Heads of News and Current Affairs of both the English and French networks.

Chapter 10: The Conservative Style

1. James Moore, "Evidence", Standing Committee on Canadian Heritage, May 29, 2012, [http://www.parl.gc.ca/HousePublications/Publication.aspx?DocId=5615160&Language=E].
2. Everyone, Every Way. Five-Year Strategic Plan, CBC/Radio-Canada, 2015, [www.cbc.radio-canada.ca/_files/cbcrc/documents/strategie-2015/document-2015-2-pager-fr.pdf].
3. The similar and beloved *Dispatches* on CBC Radio had already been cancelled in June 2012.
4. The Local Program Improvement Fund, financed by the broadcast distribution undertakings, was created by the CRTC in 2008 and disappeared in September 2014. The funds were available to both the public and private broadcasters. In total, it provided access to about $100 million a year.
5. Patrice Côté, "Minorité francophone: Radio-Canada soutient être

consciente de son role" ["Radio-Canada affirms that it is aware of its role with regard to francophone minorities"], *L'Acadie nouvelle* (February 27, 2014) [www.acadienouvelle.com/actualites/2014/02/27/minorite-franco-phone-radio-canada-soutient-etre-consciente-de-son-role/].

6. Proceedings of the Standing Committee on Transport and Communications, February 26, 2014, http://www.parl.gc.ca/content/sen/committee/412%5CTRCM/03EV-51227-E.HTM.

7. Ibid.

8. Patrick Beauduin was managing director of French Radio from November 2010 until May 2013. No longer employed by Radio-Canada, he works as a consultant.

9. Anne Sérode was head of the Première Chaîne from March 2011 until May 2013. She is now in charge of programming at France Bleu Roussillon.

10. Radio-Canada news release, August 17, 2011.

11. Anne Sérode, telephone interview with the author, April 3, 2014.

12. Patrick Beauduin, telephone interview with the author, April 3, 2014.

13. Patrick Beauduin, email to the author, April 3, 2014.

14. Anne Sérode, email to the author, July 19, 2014.

15. Hubert Lacroix, CBC/Radio-Canada, August 6, 2010.

16. See Chapters 4 and 5.

17. Centre d'études sur les médias, Rapport intermédiaire, June 2011. At the time, we had not yet received the centre's final report, but its conclusions were unchanged from those of the interim report.

18. Expenses, request A-2011-00082, travel number 250002206, 218 [http://www.cbc.radio-canada.ca/_files/cbcrc/documents/ati/a201100082.pdf].

19. This was Jean Pelletier, who was mayor of Quebec City from 1977 to 1989 and chief of staff to Jean Chrétien for eleven years. He died in January 2009. Eddie Goldenberg was Prime Minister Jean Chrétien's principal political advisor.

20. Robert Rabinovitch, email to the author, February 23, 2014.

21. Commission of Inquiry into the Awarding and Management of Public Contracts in the Construction Industry, interview report, File #2010-11-004.

22. "Advertising on CBC/Radio-Canada services must not create the perception that CBC/Radio-Canada programs and Web services are being influenced by advertising or sponsorship messages scheduled in or adjacent to them. It must always be clear to audiences when products, services or points of view are being advertised." CBC Advertising Standards [http://www.cbc.radio-canada.ca/en/reporting-to-canadians/acts-and-policies/programming/advertising-standards/].

23. Lise Payette, "Stephen Harper va s'en laver les mains" ["Stephen Harper will

wash his hands of it"], *Le Devoir*, May 30, 2014, [www.ledevoir.com/politique/canada/409589/stephen-harper-va-s-en-laver-les-mains].

24. "Accepting free travel to help in newsgathering, creation of content or for research puts us in a conflict of interest. The provisions of CBC's policy on free travel are covered in Corporate Policy 1.1.2: http://www.cbc.radio-canada.ca/docs/policies/program/free.shtml." [http://www.cbc.radio-canada.ca/en/reporting-to-canadians/acts-and-policies/programming/journalism/conflict/].

25. "Production personnel will not accept offers of free travel or accommodation from outside organizations or individuals to facilitate the gathering of program, news or research material. CBC/Radio-Canada programs must be protected from improper external influence or the suspicion of such influence. Travel and accommodation costs are a form of program expense. They are not to be absorbed by outside agencies for News and current affairs programs under the CBC/Radio-Canada Journalistic Standards and Practices." [http://www.cbc.radio-canada.ca/en/reporting-to-canadians/acts-and-policies/programming/program-policies/1-1-12/].

26. See the Government of Canada site The War of 1812, and in particular the "Heroes of the War of 1812" page [http://1812.gc.ca/eng/1317828221939/1317828660198].

27. André Pratte, "Caricaturer 1812" ["Caricaturing 1812"], *La Presse* (October 12, 2011) [www.lapresse.ca/debats/editoriaux/andre-pratte/201110/12/01-4456365-caricaturer-1812.php].

28. "Hommage à Alain Saulnier en direct à RDI" ["Homage to Alain Saulnier live on RDI"], February 23, 2012 [youtube/5720tWH0A54].

29. Canada Newswire, "Government of Canada Announces Reappointment to CBC/Radio-Canada," October 5, 2012, [http://www.prnewswire.com/news-releases/government-of-canada-announces-reappointment-to-cbcradio-canada-172884241.html].

30. Rémi Racine, chair of the board of CBC/Radio-Canada, letter to the board, October 5, 2012, translated from French.

31. Quoted by Stéphane Baillargeon, "ICI retrouve Radio-Canada" ["ICI returns to Radio-Canada"], *Le Devoir* (June 11, 2013) [www.ledevoir.com/societe/medias/380441/ici-retrouve-radio-canada].

32. Francine Pelletier, "Ici Radio-Compression", *Le Devoir* (May 14, 2014) [www.ledevoir.com/societe/medias/408170/ici-radio-compression].

33. Government of Canada, "Statement by the Minister of Canadian Heritage, Shelly Glover, about CBC/Radio-Canada", June 26, 2014, [http://news.gc.ca/web/article-en.do?nid=862569&_ga=1.19043965.415389600.1429285560].

Chapter 11: The Great Dismantling

1. Lise Payette, "Stephen Harper va s'en laver les mains" ["Stephen Harper will wash his hands of it"], *Le Devoir*.
2. Jim Abbott was a Member of Parliament from 1993 to 2011. For details, see Chapter 8.
3. CBC/Radio-Canada, *A Space for Us All*.
4. Marc Cassivi, "Le plus inquiétant" ["The most worrisome"], *La Presse*, April 22, 2014, [www.lapresse.ca/debats/chroniques/marc-cassivi/201404/22/01-4759636-le-plus-inquietant.php].
5. CBC/Radio-Canada, *A Space for Us All*, 8.
6. CBC/Radio-Canada, Social Responsibility and Public Value at CBC/Radio-Canada. Citizenship: Inside and Out, [http://www.public-value.cbc.radio-canada.ca/].
7. CB/Radio-Canada, *A Space for Us All*. The document is no longer available on CBC's website, but it is available here: https://www.friends.ca/news-item/9989.
8. The Committee hearing transcript is here: http://www.parl.gc.ca/HousePublications/Publication.aspx?DocId=6560939&Language=E&Mode=1&Parl=41&Ses=2.
9. Ibid.
10. See the anecdote in Chapter 8.
11. CBC/Radio-Canada, *A Space for Us All*, 1.
12. Ibid. 10.
13. Alain Saulnier, "Compressions à Radio-Canada. Refuser la lente mise à mort d'une grande institution" ["Budget cuts at Radio-Canada. Refuse the slow putting to death of a great institution"], *Le Devoir*, April 14, 2014 [media1.ledevoir.com/societe/medias/405464/compressions-].
14. Konrad Yakabuski, "Don't Make Radio-Canada Subsidize the CBC", the *Globe and Mail*, July 14, 2014 [www.theglobeandmail.com/globe-debate/dont-make-radio-canada-subsidize-the-cbc/article19571573/].
15. Jason Lynch, "Charts: How We Watch TV Now", Quartz, July 21, 2014, [qz.com/237600/charts-how-we-watch-tv-now/]. The article reports on a news conference by David Poltrack, Chief Research Officer at CBS.
16. Éric Scherer, "Recherche confiance, désespérément!" ["Desperately seeking confidence!"], Méta-Média, May 8, 2014 [meta-media.fr/2014/05/08/recherche-confiance-desesperement.html]. Scherer is director of the future, digital, and international strategy linked to new media, France Télévisions.
17. Google, "About Google" [https://www.google.ca/intl/en/about/].
18. "Facebook a conduit une expérience secrète sur 700000 utilisateurs" ["Facebook conducted a secret experiment on 700,000 users"] Le Figaro.fr, June 30,

2014, [www.lefigaro.fr/secteur/high-tech/2014/06/30/01007-20140630ART FIG00096-facebook-a-conduit-une-experience-secrete-sur-700000-utilisateurs.php]. For the original article, see Adam D. I. Kramer, Jamie E. Guillory, and Jeffrey T. Hancock, "Experimental Evidence of Massive-Scale Emotional Contagion Through Social Networks", Proceedings of the National Academy of Sciences of the United States of America (PNAS), [www.pnas.org/content/111/24/8788.abstract?sid=f44a 1d23-42e5-42bc-9f65-ac8d62d055d2].

19. Éric Scherer, "Recherche, confiance, désespérément!"

20. Dr Werner Rumphorst, "Comment garantir l'indépendance de la télévision de service public?" ["How to Guarantee the Independence of Public Service Television?"] Budapest, November 3, 2006.

21. CBC/Radio-Canada, Journalistic Standards and Practices.

INDEX

Index

ALSO FROM DUNDURN

Irresponsible Government
Brent Rathgeber

Irresponsible Government examines the current state of Canadian democracy in contrast to the founding principles of responsible government established by the Fathers of Confederation in 1867. The book examines the failure of modern elected representatives to perform their constitutionally mandated duty to hold the prime minister and his cabinet to account. It further examines the modern lack of separation between the executive and legislative branches of government and the disregard with which the executive views Parliament. The book seeks to shine light on the current power imbalances that have developed in Canadian government.

Through an examination of the foundation principles of our parliamentary system and their subsequent erosion, *Irresponsible Government* seeks methods through which we can begin to recalibrate and correct these power imbalances and restore electoral accountability.

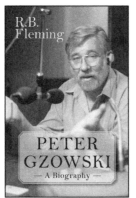

Peter Gzowski: A Biography
R.B. Fleming

Born in 1934, Peter Gzowski covered most of the last half of the century as a journalist and interviewer. This biography, the most comprehensive and definitive yet published, is also a portrait of Canada during those decades, beginning with Gzowski's days at the University of Toronto's *The Varsity* in the mid-1950s, through his years as the youngest-ever managing editor of *Maclean's* in the 1960s and his tremendous success on CBC's *Morningside* in the 1980s and 1990s, and ending with his stint as a *Globe and Mail* columnist at the dawn of the 21st century and his death in January 2002.

Gzowski saw eight Canadian Prime Ministers in office, most of whom he interviewed, and witnessed everything from the Quiet Revolution in Quebec to the growth of economic nationalism in Canada's West. From the rise of state medicine to the decline of the patriarchy, Peter was there to comment, to resist, and to participate. Here was a man who was proud to call himself Canadian and who made millions of other Canadians realize that Canada was, in what he claimed was a Canadian expression, not a bad place to live.